28 SHARE MARKET MONEY MAKING SECRETS

28 SHARE MARKET MONEY MAKING SECRETS

SUDHA SHRIMALI

Ocean Books
Pvt. Ltd.

Published by

Ocean Books (P) Ltd.

4/19 Asaf Ali Road,
New Delhi-110 002 (INDIA)
e-mail: prabhatbooks@gmail.com

ISBN 978-81-8430-638-5

28 SHARE MARKET MONEY MAKING SECRETS

by Sudha Shrimali

Edition

First, 2022

Price

₹ 300.00 (Three Hundred Rupees only)

Printed at

AMSONS, Sahibabad

To

All those millions of Indian investors,

who rely on stock market profits

for their future plans

Contents

1

Story of the Stock Market

Formation in 1875 as an Association

The Mumbai stock market was established in the year 1875 as an association with the name 'The Native Share & Stock Brokers Association'. Trading in stocks had already started even before that. The stockbrokers used to gather together under a tree to trade in stocks. The idea of forming an association took shape there only and that only culminated in a historical event. India was under British rule at that time. The words spoken on 18 January 1899 by the British High Commissioner J. S. McLean for the native stockbrokers are remembered with pride even today. The substance of McLean's point of view was that the native stockbrokers of Mumbai were inseparable part of the society and instead of giving them the recognition they deserved, they were being evaluated on their demerits only. Save for some exceptions, these stockbrokers have continued to be trustworthy. They have always paid back every penny of their customers, irrespective of the quantum of loss suffered by them. This is the largest capital market in India. It has been instrumental in uplifting organisations like the Mumbai Port Trust and the Mumbai Municipality. Presently, these native stockbrokers play a significant role in building Mumbai. This notion has remained true for Mumbai stockbrokers even in this 21st century. Of course, exceptions in some form or measure do keep appearing every now and then.

First Stock Exchange of the World

It is believed that the first stock market of the world was established in Belgium. Many traders had gathered together in Antwerp city of Belgium in the year 1531 for major expansion of the market. They speculated in stocks and commodities. The first organised stock exchange of the world was established in the year 1602 in Amsterdam. The New York Stock Exchange, recognised as one of the mightiest exchanges of the world, came into existence towards the end of 18th century. During that period, it was an accepted common practice among business class in India to trade in Hundis and bills of exchange.

Banyan Tree and Stock Exchange

Trading in stocks in any market is determined by their demand and supply. The stock exchange that maintains records of this kind of trades is considered to be the barometer of economy. It is believed that the first stock market of the world was opened around 1531 in the city of Antwerp in Belgium. However, the first stock market in a formal shape was established in the year 1602 in the city of Amsterdam in Netherlands. In India, the first organised stock exchange came into existence in 1875 in the form of an association of local brokers in Mumbai. It was named as 'The Native Share & Stock Brokers Association'. Before establishment of this association, these brokers used to get together under a banyan tree to trade in stocks. This unorganised market of stocks had started functioning in India around 1840 only. The BSE was also conceived under this very banyan tree. This banyan tree was located somewhere near the Town Hall close to the present Horniman Circle. Incidentally, the brokers kept changing their place of operation based on their number and needs and finally, it was in the year 1874 when they got a permanent place for themselves. This very place is now known as 'Dalal Street'.

Later, a stock exchange was established in Ahmedabad in the year 1894. Stocks of local textile industry units were traded in this exchange. Kolkata also got a stock exchange in 1908. The World War II had a major impact on the development of stock exchanges. India had only 7 stock exchanges in 1939 when the War started and by the time the War ended in 1945, this number had swelled to 21. Today, 24 stock exchanges are operational in India. These exchanges in India are provided recognition under Securities Contracts (Regulation) Act, 1956. Subsequently, these exchanges are classified in three categories A, B and C based on various criteria.

Treasure of Knowledge on Hindi Website of BSE

BSE has made available a special facility for Hindi speaking investors. On its website 'hindi.bseindia.com', major announcements made by various companies and the exchange are made available to you in Hindi right from morning till late night. Not only that, this site also has valuable information for guidance of investors. This website of BSE also provides every evening the details of stock market trends that you normally find in newspapers next day or on TV news in the night. Additionally, the website contains a great deal of significant information and statistics that are very helpful to investors in taking their investment decisions.

First Share Mania

The Government of India, in the year 1850, passed the Companies Act, 1850 that paved the way for a new method of stock trading. It was new because before this, the level of trading in stocks was just nominal. It was not possible for this trading to pick up speed without availability of stocks in large numbers. The stocks available for trade those days were limited to those of some major banks like Commercial Bank, Chartered Bank, The Oriental Bank and Bank of Bombay. People also were not so interested in making investment in stocks. Minimal records were maintained for stock trade transactions and only six stockbrokers were managing the entire operation. There was neither a trading hall nor any building for stock market. Even the capital required for the same was not available. Despite all this, the number of stockbrokers went up to 60 by the year 1860. The year 1860 saw the emergence of a person who was responsible for the advent of 'Share Mania'. His name was Premchand Roychand. He was the first Indian stockbroker who could read and write English.

Premchand Roychand was instrumental in setting up several companies including land reclamation companies. People's inclination towards stock trading started to show upward trend and, as a consequence, the number of stockbrokers also went up to somewhere between 200 and 250. Later, with the end of the American Civil War in 1865, the inflow of capital that was required for development of the market in India declined and 'Share Mania' came to an end. The stock prices tumbled down dramatically overnight. Consequently, the business of stockbrokers came to a halt. This gave rise to the idea of an association of stockbrokers in their mind and these stockbrokers came together to form an unofficial association between 1868 and 1873. In the year 1874, these stockbrokers found a site for carrying our regular trades and that is famous as 'Dalal Street' today.

On 3 December 1887, the stockbrokers gave this association a formal shape and 'The Native Share & Stock Brokers Association' came into being. Thus, the entity of Stock Market, Mumbai was established in July 1875 with only 318 individuals as members, each of them paying a membership fee of Re 1 only. They passed a resolution to construct a hall or a building to be used by the members of the association for safeguarding the interest, position and complexion of the native share and stockbrokers. No action could be taken on this resolution until 1887. However, a trust deed was certainly created and the words written in this trust deed in 1887 became the foundation stones of the present Stock Market in Mumbai. This is how the famous great institution in the form of Bombay Stock Exchange (B.S.E.) came into being with the sincere efforts of these people. Thus, the journey that started under a tree is today moving ahead on the path of progress by securing a significant place on the global platform in the form of a modern corporate entity. This organised stock trading was launched in the 18th century by the British East India Company with trading in term papers issued for its various ventures and for collection of funds; trading in shares of the banks like Commercial Bank and Mercantile Bank of Bombay also started with the same.

❑❑

2

What is a Stock Market?

News items sometimes like 'Historical bounce of 1000 points in the stock market' and 'Investors get richer by ₹2 lakh crores' or other times like 'Stock market crashes by 1000 points' and 'Investors wealth wiped out massively' give rise to different kinds of questions in the minds of common people as to why stock markets undergo such sudden ups and downs? What actually happens on a particular day that creates such chaos involving thousands of crores of rupees? Awakened readers should realise that the stock market does have such inherent behaviour and that's the reason its index is known as 'SENSEX' i.e. sensitive index. It's because of its sensitivity that it fluctuates with the impact of news of various incidents happening in the country and all around the world. The Sensex just needs some excuse to move up or down and the market remains still when it does not find any. But, who at all would be interested in such a stagnant market?

The stock market surely is volatile but it should not be treated just as a speculative market because of its volatility. There is definitely some speculation but there is a separate stadium for every player in this market. For day traders (day traders are people who constantly keep buying and selling stocks the whole day), this is just casino gambling whereas for those who just remain in the market for investment, this is a pure investment market. It is safer to be in this market as an investor; his investment not only remains safe but may also create more wealth.

We may try to understand this with the help of some true stories. Had an individual invested ₹10000 in Wipro in the year 1980 and held on to the same until 2006, the value of his investment would have grown to ₹200 crores. Similarly, had a person invested ₹10000 in the first public issue of Reliance Industries of Dhirubhai Ambani, the same would have grown to ₹2 crores by now. In short, the investors who select good companies and remain invested in them for long periods reap huge profits. Stocks may be bought anytime for long term investment. This is because it is the fundamental characteristics of this market that amply favours those who remain patient.

What is an IPO?

'Initial Public Offer' (IPO) refers to the process by which

a company, in order to raise capital, offers its shares to the public for the first time. The shares that are allotted to applicants after a public issue may be bought and sold in the stock market after listing of the company. The trades in such shares after listing are referred to as 'secondary market'. When a company offers its shares to existing shareholders, the same is called a Rights Issue. The shareholders have the privilege to apply for new shares in the company in a specified proportion to their existing shareholdings. However, they don't have any compulsion to apply for such new shares. When a company constantly makes profit, it generally keeps distributing a portion of the profit every year to the shareholders as dividends. When the remaining portions of the profit get accumulated and the same is capitalised by issuing fresh shares free-of-cost to the existing shareholders in a fixed proportion to their existing holdings, the same is referred to as 'Bonus Share'.

Be Careful while Applying for IPO

While applying for an IPO of a company, the investor should find out some basic details about the company. Who are the promoters of the company? How is the track record of the promoters? If these promoters are involved in any other company or companies, how are their financial results? Which industrial sector does the company belong to? What is the current state of that industry and what are its future prospects? What are the future plans of the company?

How good are its projected working results? Answers to many such questions may be found in the offer document (Prospectus) of the company. This document also provides details of the risk factors of the company. Now, companies are required to get their IPO graded. This grading is assigned by many grading companies including CRISIL. This grading is assigned on a five-point scale from 1 to 5 based on the fundamentals of the company. The company with score of 1 is considered to be weak on fundamentals. It is better to avoid such companies for investment in their issues. Grades 2 and 3 indicate better companies. Companies with grades 4 and 5 have strong fundamentals and outstanding positions.

Significance of PAN in Stock Markets

This needs to be understood clearly that now that the Income Tax Permanent Account Number (PAN) is necessary for entering into any transaction for investment in stock markets and also for making an application for IPO. Similarly, a Demat account is also required for trading in stock markets. And a Demat account can't be opened without PAN card. Thus, any deal in stocks is now not possible without PAN number. However, you don't need to panic on hearing the name of Income Tax PAN. Transparency in respect of Income Tax has already improved in this age of computers and hence, investors handling transactions in stocks don't have to worry much. The government is still keeping the dividends on shares tax-free, meaning that the amount that a company pays out of its profit to its shareholders in the form of dividends every year does not attract any income tax.

Besides above, the government has also extended many other tax benefits to the investors investing in stock markets. When a shareholder makes a profit by selling his share within a period of 12 months from the date of its purchase, that profit is treated as short term capital gains. This is called 'Long Term Capital Gains' and the same does not attract any tax. This means that no tax is applicable on the profit that an investor makes by selling his shares more than 12 months after their dates of purchase.

Stock Market Details

A large group of investors still have doubts about the difference between BSE and NSE. Not only that, who are being served by the stock markets located in different states and how are they different from the above two? BSE (Bombay Stock Exchange) and NSE (National Stock Exchange) are fully computerised online stock exchanges.

The BSE is the largest stock exchange not only in the country but also in entire Asia. It has the maximum number of listed companies. On the other hand, it has been only 17 years since the NSE was established. Both of them are global level stock exchanges and its members may enter into trades at these exchanges from anywhere in the country. On the contrary, the stock markets in various states have lost volumes and the number of trades being carried out in those markets is negligible. Not only that, these stock markets are almost closed and they carry out trades on BSE and NSE after securing their memberships.

What are Sensex and other Indexes?

Whenever there is a talk of stock market, the first word that is heard or read is 'Sensex'. The headlines like 'Sensex has crossed 20000 level' or 'Sensex crashed' keep on appearing in newspapers or on TV channels. The Sensex is the benchmark index of BSE and incorporates 30 blue chip companies in 12 major industrial sectors. Hence, this is considered to be the barometer of fluctuations in the market. Ups and downs in the Sensex reflect booms and slumps respectively in the market.

When somebody invests in a company included in the Sensex, he has the confidence that the company he is putting his money in is quite strong from the point of view of its fundamentals and growth prospects. If you feel that the Sensex is going to rise, you may enter into Futures contracts for buying the same, and if you expect a fall in the Sensex, you may write contracts to sell the same. Such deals are known as 'Sensex Futures Contracts'. Even 'Mini Futures Contracts' have been launched to allow BSE investors to enter into Sensex Futures deals with limited capital investment.

Choice of Broker

Investment in a stock market can be done only through

registered stockbrokers. Investors should carefully choose a broker and take into account not only his track record, quality of his service, consultation services for customers, research etc. but also his dealings with you before finalising a broker. It's not proper to select a broker just because he provides cheaper services or charges lower brokerage or provides attractive and tempting news.

Similarly, you need a Depository Participant (DP) for opening a Demat account. A broker or even a bank can be your DP. If you have faith in your broker, you may even get a Demat account opened through him in a nearby bank. Currently, many of the banks are providing the facility of a Trading Account also along with the Demat account. You need to provide details of your Demat account, PAN card number, photograph, address proof, bank account etc. while opening a Trading account. Transparency in this entire process is constantly improving.

Arithmetic of Tips

You come across the word 'Tips' quite frequently in a stock market. People keep on telling each other which of the stocks are going to double in three months or something like that. In the language of the market, this kind of advice is termed as 'Tips'. Operators and speculators promote this tips-culture on a large scale; this keeps feeding the market even information based on lies and rumours. Investors should always remain wary of such tips spreading in the market.

This tips-culture becomes more prominent during market booms. These tips do not have any sound background and hence the quantum of risk in trades based on such tips is quite high. It is often observed that new investors get induced by such tips and make investments based on them only to repent later for consequent loss.

❑❑

3

New Investors: Problems & Solutions

How to Select a Stockbroker?

Both BSE and NSE have lists of brokers displayed on their websites. Additionally, brokers also keep publishing their own details through various mediums. However, it's important to check the track record before choosing a stockbroker and selection becomes a bit comfortable if the broker is located near your residence or office. These days, even many banks are in the business of brokering and you may even choose one of them.

Whom to Select as Depository Participant (DP)?

As far as possible, avail this service from your broker only if he is providing the same. Alternatively, you may choose somebody providing DP service near your residence or office. Most of the banks are depository participants. You may choose to open your Demat account with one of them. Please take care to keep record of your Demat account and information relating to the same properly. Please keep your instruction slips carefully.

What To Do if you Have a Complaint Against any Company, Broker or DP?

The Investors Services Department of the stock market and even SEBI may be contacted for complaints against companies. Complaints against brokers may be lodged with the stock market and if the response from the stock market is not satisfactory, the same may even be escalated to SEBI. Complaints against DPs should be lodged with the depository. Even in this case, SEBI only is the last resort.

What are the Sources for Company Information?

Business channels, newspapers and companies engaged in financial review keep on providing news about companies. Besides that, various news right from working results to other developments related to the companies are also regularly provided on the website of the stock market. Information about companies may also be found on their own websites. Information related to research reports of independent research agencies and brokers also keep on getting published from time to time. The latest news about companies keep appearing even on TV news channels.

What is the Process for Opening an Account with Stockbroker or DP?

As a customer, you need to provide all the information to your stockbroker and you have to sign a contract. The broker then provides you a 'Unique Identification Number'. Similarly, you have to provide your details to the DP also. Most importantly, it is necessary to provide your Income Tax PAN (Permanent Account) number to open these accounts. It's not possible to open accounts with broker or DP without the same. PAN has become essential now for trading in stock markets or holding stocks.

❑❑

4

Stories of Upheavals in Stock Markets

Day: Monday, 21 January 2008.

Location: Dalal Street, Mumbai.

There is gloom on every face here. Some people are completely ruined. People who were multimillionaires yesterday are having empty coffers today. This day of massive upheaval in the stock market would be known as the 'Black Monday' for Indian stock markets. The market crashed by 1408.35 points on this day. This was the biggest-ever intra-day loss in the history. We may understand the impact if we measure this loss in Indian currency. The stock market wiped out crores of rupees of investors on a single day. The impact was felt by everybody, right from a small trader to a large capitalist. Everybody had his own opinion markets for this crash in Indian stock market. The situation looked so hopeless that it prompted stockbrokers to protest against SEBI. This 'Black Monday' shook the stock markets not only in Mumbai but also all around the world. Even many of the indexes considered to be strong crashed to the ground the moment they opened. The fall in index was not anticipated and the entire week was to remain disappointing for the stock market.

Whereas the media all across the world was crying hoarse on this crash, this was nothing more than exciting news for a common man. Most of the people could not understand the significance of such a huge loss. The distance maintained by common people from the world of stock markets prevented them from appreciating the impact of this disaster and this tsunami of the stock market could not connect people's sympathy to the experts, as the common man regarded all these just as a gamble. A common man knows very little about this world and nurtures quite a few preconceptions. Even though the information-revolution has made its vocabulary quite popular, general people are still not much aware of its real significance. A lot of questions relating to stock markets keep arising in the mind of people. Answers to these questions may be found in the success of a common investor. Let us try to understand the same with the story of a common investor named Hiren Bhai.

❑❑

5

A True Story of a Common Man Turning Special

The common man will have to understand the story of Hiren Bhai to unravel the complex puzzle of the stock market. This story has one more character named Viren Bhai who is an industrialist and whose company has a good reputation in the stock market. This is the success story of a common man like Hiren Bhai growing to match or even surpass Viren Bhai. As mentioned above, Hiren Bhai is a common man having a modest job. His income is enough to fulfil the needs of his family, but he feels that an additional source of income is required to make his life happier. He finds stock market as an option for additional income; however, he is hesitant to invest there, as he does not have any knowledge of this field. He hence approaches a stock market expert to find a solution to this problem. He wants to understand what exactly a share is and how can he benefit from investing in the same.

Small Owner of a Big Company

Share means 'to give something to others'. In fact, this process involves distribution only. Possibly, Viren Bhai may explain this better. Viren Bhai is a well-known businessman and possesses good experience in trading. He wants to expand his business. He does not have enough capital for this expansion, though he does have a good action plan for the same. He may not get advance even from banks for such a large investment. Hence, he has only one option to raise capital - to make common people partners in his project. He issues 'shares' to common people to become partners in his project. The share here actually means an offer of partnership from his company that can be bought at a specified price. Thus, a common man may, depending on the capital available with him, buy partnership in that company and become a partner in its profit. Hiren Bhai would make his investment in such a small company only as a junior partner. But here is the next question from Hiren Bhai - there must be some conditions for that partnership; do they have different kinds of shares based on those conditions?

Kinds of Partnerships

Hiren Bhai may buy two kinds of shares from a public limited company. The first is known as 'Preferential Share' and the second one as 'Equity Share'.

1. Preferential Share

Preferential share provides Hiren Bhai the benefit of receiving a fixed dividend. Holders of this kind of shares are paid dividends first, before common dividends are issued. This shareholder i.e. Hiren Bhai is not considered a partner of the company. Based on the profit, there are three kinds of Preferential shares as below.

a. **Non-cumulative Preferential Share:** If the company does not make any profit during a year but earns profit next year, Hiren Bhai as a holder of this share, can't claim to receive dividends for both the years.

b. **Cumulative Preferential Share:** If the organisation or the company does not make any profit during a year but earns profit next year, Hiren Bhai as a holder of this share, can claim to receive dividends for both the years.

c. **Redeemable Cumulative Preferential Share:** The holder of this share is repaid his entire investment along with dividends after a fixed period. Association of this kind of shareholders with the company is entirely temporary and depends on the wish of the company.

2. Equity Share

This share is also commonly known as ordinary share. Equity only determines the partnership in any company. In fact, an equity shareholder is directly linked to the interest and problems of the company and its profit and loss have direct impact on him. Once Hiren Bhai buys this kind of a share, his profit gets linked to that company's profit. If the company incurs loss, the price of its shares gets impacted and that results in loss to Hiren Bhai. When the company earns profit, Hiren Bhai also makes money. This is also defined as a membership to the company and provides the right to advise and vote on the company's decisions.

The point to be noted is that dividends are distributed to equity shareholders only after distribution of dividends to preferential shareholders. Nowadays, the word 'share' is generally meant to refer to 'equity share' only.

Benefits of Bonus Share

Hiren Bhai's company has earned huge profits this year. Hence, a lot of amount is still left with the company even after distributing dividends. In order to distribute this amount, the same is converted into equity shares and then distributed among existing shareholders in proportion to their current holdings. These very additional shares are known as 'Bonus Shares'. This process does not result in any increase in the number of shareholders, but Hiren Bhai's share-holding goes up. The biggest benefit of this bonus share issue is that no tax has to be paid to the government on additional profit.

Case of Rights Issue

The company where Hiren Bhai has invested proposes to

issue fresh shares but does not want to increase the number of shareholders. In such a case, the company issues new shares to the existing shareholders only in proportion of their current share holdings. These new shares are offered to the shareholders at current record price or even at a price lower than the current market price. These very shares are referred to as 'Rights Issue'.

Market Reputation and Market Value

There are two kinds of markets based on the trades handled. Every company issues its shares in the Primary Market only. All the activities right from issue to allotment and listing are carried out in this market only. Every share is assigned a fixed price that is determined by the company promoters like Viren Bhai. The company issues its shares in the primary market on this very price. All subsequent trades in these shares take place in a secondary market. Just to put this straight, if Hiren Bhai buys his shares directly from the company, the transaction takes place in the primary market. In the secondary market, these shares are traded at prices higher than the issue price. This depends on the market reputation of the company. The better is the reputation of the company, the more is the market price of its shares. After getting the feel of shares, Hiren Bhai had some more queries. Where are these shares traded? How are they traded?

In other words, what is a share market or stock market and how does the same work?

Juggling in Market

We are treating Viren Bhai as head of a company that is approaching market to raise capital. Viren Bhai or any other company who wants to issue shares will have to go through a stock market to sell those shares. New and old securities and shares are traded in a stock market. Viren Bhai would raise his capital by selling his shares through the stock market and his enterprise would be recognised as a public limited company. Every public limited company has its shares listed in a stock exchange. The persons or entities launching this kind of enterprise are known as company promoters. Viren Bhai is the promoter of his company. The number of promoters may even be more. These promoters only decide the rules for the company. Even the number, percentage, price etc. for the shares are determined by these promoters. After a company is formed, it has to be registered with the Registrar of Companies. Only after that, the company gets the right to issue shares or debentures. There is a big difference between a share and a debenture. A share provides ownership in a company whereas a debenture involves payment of interest in a definite mode. Shareholders are paid dividends based on the profit earned by the company.

Initial Phase of Hiren Bhai

After having gathered so much information about stock markets, Hiren Bhai was now in a position to start his investment. He was however still in a state of hesitation, trying to figure out how to make a start. Some of his old friends who were already familiar with this market suggested Hiren Bhai to open a Demat account. They told him that it was not possible to buy shares without a Demat account. This was an essential requirement for investment in stock market. It was now necessary for Hiren Bhai to find out what this Demat account was and what was required to maintain the same.

Account without a Bank

Just as you need a bank account to operate on your money and keep the same safe, you require a Demat account to trade in shares in the stock market. Demat refers to 'Dematerialisation'. This indicates that you have received the property of a company in a non-verbal or non-apparent mode. The Demat account scheme has been made available to keep a record of such transactions only. This has also been introduced to eliminate the risks of the property being fake or bogus or even getting stolen that are associated with such transactions being carried out in a physical form. In fact, this is similar to a bank account with money replaced by shares. You would have to approach the nearest depository to open your Demat account. A Demat account eliminates the requirement of original certificates. The account gets updated as and when you buy or sell shares.

The Riddle of Depository

Ever since the stock market scam of 1992, the government was looking for a way out to regulate stock trading and keep a watch over the same. Keeping that only in mind, it was decided to introduce Depository Receipt Mechanism sans physical exchange of share certificates. No certificate of any kind is required to be held under this scheme to prove ownership of shares. Its objective is basically to maintain the record of ownership rights. SEBI has registered two depository companies - National Securities Depository Ltd (NSDL) and Central Depository Services (India) Ltd (CDSIL) under the Depositories Act. These two depositories only maintain Demat accounts.

Hiren Bhai had by now understood that the way to the stock market passed through the Demat account. He successfully opened a Demat account. Many entities right from small brokers to many large companies investing in the stock market facilitate opening of Demat accounts. Hiren Bhai, after opening his Demat account, was faced with another big question - which companies to invest in so as to earn good returns in a safe way? He then approached a broker for this. A broker works as a bridge between the buyer and the seller of shares and ensures conclusion of all their deals in the stock market.

Investment Strategy

Every exchange keeps a watch over its trading activities. Hence, it is necessary that all buying and selling be carried out through a specific channel or source that the exchange is aware of and that is also committed to provide information to the exchange. Brokers function as this very channel. Every person who wishes to become a broker has to first of all get himself registered with the exchange where he wants to carry out his activities. Once registered, he is officially entitled to buy and sell shares in the exchange. Any person may take the broker's help to buy or sell shares and the broker receives some amount as commission for his services. The broker provides record of all such transactions to the exchange. Hiren Bhai received some suggestions from the broker and accordingly, after thinking over the same for few days, he divided his capital into three parts. He invested the first part in reputed and blue chip stocks.

Savings in Blue Chips

Famous and well-recognised companies who have a long history of sound performance, are progressing well and have the potential for further growth in future are known as blue chip companies and their stocks are referred to as blue chip stocks. Hiren Bhai invested the second portion of his capital in mutual funds and used the third part to buy IPOs.

Profitable Mutual Funds

This is a mode of investing in stock market. In this system, large banks and investors collect money from common people and invest the same based on advice from experts. This process has the lowest probability of loss, but at the same time, it would be an improbable condition to expect 100% profit.

First Step of an IPO

This is the first step for a private company on its path to a public company. This is the first stock sale for any private company. After this, the private company converts to a public company. Mostly small and medium-sized companies use IPO, though many times even large companies have been found to use this. In this offering, a company goes to public with its plan and invites them to invest in the same. Incidentally, IPO is considered to be a risky domain as investors, especially small investors do not know how that company is going to operate in future and how would they fare in the market. Money gets blocked in this for a long time and success is also not guaranteed.

This strategy of investing in three parts has brought down the risk of loss for Hiren Bhai and improved the chances of profit. It's a pearl of wisdom in the stock market never to invest your entire capital in a single option. If you have `100, invest the same in stocks, bonds, bank deposits and other savings options. Hiren Bhai's decision proved to be fruitful. This encouraged him and he started paying attention to some bigger deals. He now had enough funds to be able to buy shares of some big companies. And finally he succeeded in doing the same. But, his broker one day informed him that Sensex had crashed and hence, the prices of his stocks had come down and he was not in a profitable position for the time being. Hiren Bhai was not able to make out why at all a fall in the Sensex had resulted in his loss. He had some questions in his mind with regard to the Sensex. He was still not able to understand the arithmetic of index, as till then he had been making decisions only based on broker's suggestions and business prospects instead of getting into any analysis on indexes.

Market Thermometer

Index is nothing but a thermometer to measure the state of a market. Index may indicate how good or bad is the demand for stocks in that stock exchange. A rising index reflects the growing strength of the market. In this situation, demand for stocks goes up and their prices also go up. A falling index in turn indicates weakness in the market when demand for stocks falls and prices of the stocks also go down. It's not the index that impacts the market; rather it gets impacted by the market.

Story of Sensex

The Sensex is an index of the Bombay Stock Exchange. This index came into existence in 1986. Its full name is Sensitive

Index. The word 'SENSEX' was for the first time used by a stock market analyst Deepak Mohoni. The Sensex is based on the stocks of 30 large companies listed on BSE. Its base year is 1978-79, meaning that its computation was started with a base value of 100 as on 1 April 1979. Just like other indexes, a rise in the Sensex signifies jump in stock prices and a fall in the same provides an indication of stock prices going down. The free-float market capitalisation method is used for computing the Sensex. This covers 30 largest companies in the market. This is the most accurate and popular methodology for computing indexes.

Arithmetic of Market Cap

Market cap of a company is the total value of its stocks. This may be understood with Viren Bhai's example. Viren Bhai has issued 10 shares of his company in the market and the current market price is ₹10000 per share. The market cap of his company can then be arrived at by multiplying the market price of its share with the number of shares issued. In simple words, the product arrived at by multiplying the market price of the share of a company with the total number of its shares is the 'market cap' of that company. Based on this very market cap, each of the companies is classified as large cap (large companies), mid cap (medium-sized companies) or small cap (small companies).

Free-float Market Cap versus Sensex

Free-float market cap for each of the 30 companies included in the Sensex is calculated. These market caps of all these companies are then totalled before making some computations. This computation is then proportionated to the base year of the Sensex. The figure arrived at after all these computations is the value of the Sensex. For example, if the Sensex figure is 4 for 100 crores, the same would be determined as 8 for 200 crores and 16 for 400 crores. A change in the market cap of a company may occur as a result of either change in the number of shares or fluctuation in the price of its shares.

Reliable Stocks

BSE has classified the stocks based on the performance of related companies. Grades like A, B1, B2, F, T, TS and Z are included in these classifications. Those in Grade Z are the least reliable stocks. Companies that do not care about their shareholders and do not make any effort to address their financial issues or do not comply with stock exchange requirements are included in Z category. It's not safe to invest in Z category companies and possibility of loss is greater in those stocks. Companies in group A are the best. They have large market capitalisations and hence it's generally safer to invest in them. After getting a feel of the Sensex and the stock market, Hiren Bhai developed curiosity to learn something more in this regard. Who keeps record of transactions running in crores of rupees generated in the market by thousands of investors like him? What if there is a fraud in such a transaction? Which is the organisation responsible for investigation of the same and keeping a watch over transactions? Whom to approach to lodge complaints? One name that flashed as an answer to all these questions was - SEBI.

Watchman of the Market: SEBI

The Securities and Exchange Board of India (SEBI) was established by the government to regulate the exchanges currently operating in the country. SEBI has been created to protect the interests of investors. This Board was formed based on the recommendations of the committee headed by S. A. Dave. This body was given statutory status through an Ordinance promulgated on 30 January 1992. SEBI has its headquarters located in Mumbai. SEBI focuses on maintaining transparency in operations in exchanges and pays attention to the interests of investors. SEBI only has the powers to make rules for protection of those interests.

All this knowledge had made it clear to Hiren Bhai that, before investing in any particular sector, it was essential to gather all information relating to the same or else, investing in the stock market would be like making a shot in the dark. After this knowledge comes experience. Advice from an experienced person is generally beneficial in this field. Hence, Hiren Bhai also kept seeking expert advice from time to time. All this led to Hiren Bhai being recognised as a prudent investor. This prudence helped him accumulate a lot of wealth. Taking advantage of his goodwill, he launched an investment company that would invest its clients' funds in stock market on a fixed commission. Experience again had its impact and Hiren Bhai was successful in this venture also. Riding on the crest of success, Hiren Bhai soon started a chemical factory. Growing on the strength of his merit, he one day came up with his offer of IPO of his company to the public. The buyer of a share was today the owner of a company and seller of stocks. This is the magic of stock market.

❑❑

6

Portfolio Management: It Keeps Investment Hot

The word 'Portfolio' is much in use these days. Before this, the word 'Savings' was more commonly used in place of portfolio. An individual keeps saving regularly a portion of his income for his future needs and security and then keeps investing these savings in various investment instruments in order to earn interest on the same as well as get the benefit of capital appreciation. In simple language, this very 'bag of savings' of an individual is what is referred to as his portfolio. This pool of savings may includes stocks, mutual funds, insurance schemes, PPF, Post Office savings, Kisan Vikas Patra, National Savings Certificate, RBI Bonds, Corporate bonds etc. However, when the word 'Portfolio' is used in reference to the stock market only, it means the bag of investments made in different companies. Now this is getting popular in the name of 'Portfolio Management Services' (PMS).

Along with the art of making money, a systematic investment of that money is also an art. A person may lose his entire hard-earned money if he fails in this art. It's to avoid that risk that people have now started to utilise Portfolio Management Services. Most of the people are not able to spare enough time out of their business or job to manage their own portfolio; but lack of time is not the only problem. Portfolio management also requires a good understanding of the same. Today, people are getting rich with various kinds of investments in capital market. The increase in number of such investments has also increased the heterogeneity and complications. As such, their management requires special skills.

The first thing that needs to be understood is what exactly are portfolio and its management. Why and how should a person create his portfolio of stocks and how should he take care of the same? In order to understand the same in simple language, let's take an example of one Rajesh Sharma who has just been allotted 300 shares each of two companies against his applications for public issues and they have been credited to his Demat account. He later bought 500 shares each of two other companies from the stock market. Getting attracted to the rising trend in stock market, he felt inclined towards accumulating more stocks and thus, he went on to buy 200 to 2000 shares of some 8 to 10 companies in the last 6 months. He invested around ₹3.50 lakhs to buy all these stocks. The market continued with an upward trend and the total value of his stocks increased to ₹5 lakhs. We may hence say that he now owns a portfolio of ₹5 lakhs. We will refer to this as Rajesh Sharma's portfolio.

Create Your Own Portfolio

Every investor may create his own portfolio - be it a collection of stocks of 2 companies only or 22 companies. It's a common saying that one should not put all the capital into a single investment, as there is always risk of losing the entire capital if that investment goes bad. For instance, if you use your entire capital for buying stocks of a single company and the stock price goes down after that, you would be deep in worries. A better option would be to create your portfolio by accumulating small chunks of stocks of different companies. The reasoning behind the same is that there is less probability of all your stocks losing their prices simultaneously in the case of a market slump. The prices of two of your stocks may go down whereas that of two of your other stocks may actually go up. Thus, the risk gets minimised by holding stocks of different companies in your portfolio. There are two kinds of PMS services. In one, you just keep the fund management informed of your purchase and sale of stocks of your choice and you receive advice and suggestions from the fund manager in this regard. The other kind of service requires you to just provide the fund manager your investment amount and the fund manager only decides the companies where that amount is to be invested. You receive returns on your investments. Whichever manager you choose for your PMS services, it is necessary for you to have full faith in his expertise. Also, there should be transparency between you and your fund manager. Mutual funds, banks, broking companies, research houses and private companies provide this very kind of services.

PMS Means Custodian of Investment

1. You are ready to invest your capital of ₹500 thousands in the stock market.
2. You lack the information and skills for the same.
3. You are unable to spare time for the same out of your busy schedule on account of your job or business.
4. You keep in touch with a portfolio manager.
5. The portfolio manager will create a portfolio of stocks based on your risk capacity and risk tolerance.
6. You will receive returns based on your portfolio.
7. Once you avail the services of a portfolio manager, you would receive returns every year and the manager would take care of rest of the worries.

8. Portfolio manager will charge a specific fee for his services.
9. This service may be utilised to reap the benefit of market booms without actually entering the stock market directly.
10. This service provides - mental peace and happiness.

Free Online Guidance

Many investment-related websites in the country also provide some great PMS services. Though these websites do not manage your fund, they do provide the facility to create your portfolio on your own. They then organise and furnish you full record of the same. For instance, if you hold different quantities of stocks of 12 to 15 different companies, you may get yourself registered on such a website for this facility. The website would also regularly provide you latest valuation of your portfolio based on current market prices. Websites like 'moneycontrol.com' and 'bseindia.com' provide this facility free of cost. Not only that, you would also be able to see on these websites important news related to the stock market and those companies, free of cost.

Easy Way of Investing

Suppose you are one of those fortunate people who have highly paid jobs. You stay with your parents. You spend adequately on clothes, food and entertainment; you are still able to save some money at the end of every month. On one side, you are worried to see your money lying idle in your savings account and on the other side, you have friends and relatives who try to ridicule you when you try to talk about investments.

Ignore all such thoughts for some time. Do you remember any incident when somebody challenged you to achieve something looking to be impossible and you successfully attained the same? You would be surely believing in the saying that you need to be expert in your job to be a winner. There may be plenty of people who would advise you not to invest in the market in the current situation and if you do attempt, they would try their best to discourage you. However, there is also no dearth of such experienced people who know the way to make money even in the current situation. Presented below are some of those very basic rules, which, if followed, may help you create a successful portfolio even in this market going through ups and downs.

Right Portfolio

The first thing to be understood properly is that there is no set formula for creating the best portfolio. Investors always face lots of uncertainties. In such a situation, the main objective is to minimise risk and maximise returns on the portfolio. The purpose of a great portfolio should be its capital appreciation and security.

Segregate your investments into different asset segments, as these different segments move in different directions when the situation changes. If the portfolio is tilted more in a specific direction with regard to financial goal or included products, it indicates a bad time.

How to Allocate?

Your age, income capacity, risk capacity and responsibilities determine what component of your capital should go to which product. There are some more questions that you should constantly keep asking yourself. What are your long term financial goals with respect to your investments? Is your investment secure and liquid? Does it assure a guaranteed return? These are the questions. Once you take a final decision about the product to invest in, you may consider the following tips from the experts:

- **Pay attention to equity:** If you look at it as a concept, equity should get more allocation. Experts believe that, instead of putting money directly into stocks, it is better to invest in equity through mutual funds, portfolio management services or private equity funds or a mixture of all three. Around 25-30% of your portfolio should be allocated to large cap equity diversified fund and systematic investment plan (SIP) should be considered for the same.

- **Debt:** Investors may consider investing in debt based mutual funds or in bonds of reputed companies or AAA rated firms. The other options available under this segment are fixed deposits, government securities and income funds. Debt products are considered to be safe bets in portfolio. However, if you have only a few years left in your job, the decision to make smaller investment in equity and larger investment in debt does not present a possibility of better returns in the current market environment.

- **Gold and Real Estate:** Though both gold and real estate are good means of investment, investors should consider financial products or derivatives in this segment. Gold ETFs are relatively more liquid and also eliminate the risk associated with holding jewellery and coins. Real estate funds may have lock-in periods that need to be kept in mind.

Freshen up your Portfolio

There are also some tips for the people who have burnt their fingers by investments before they dived into the stock market. It's not proper to run away from the market immediately. If a person is capable of bringing in fresh capital, he should do that and segregate his investment into different segments in a way that provides good potential for great returns. It would be better for the investor to keep adjusting his portfolio based on his age, risk taking capacity and his fund requirements.

❑❑

7

Which Investment Option is Fit For You?

A lump sum investment in the stock market is considered to be a difficult decision. Investors are always careful while making their first investment in the stock market for even an amount somewhere between ₹1000 and ₹10000. At the same time, a lot of risk is involved in an investment of a large amount like ₹5-10 lakhs. The reason behind this fear is the possibility of your entire capital getting lost.

That kind of situation may be avoided by following a definite strategy. To understand the circumstances properly, let's take the example of a 35-years old individual who has `5 lakh to invest. He has three options for investment. He may put his entire amount either in stocks or mutual funds or both.

Stocks

All the fund managers generally advise investors to invest in instalments. Making a lump sum investment in one go may be dangerous. Hence, investment experts recommend an investment ratio of 60:40 or 50:50 depending on one's risk profile.

There is even a strategic segment in portfolio where long term investments provide better returns. Long term and strategic investments should be held at least for three years. At the same time, investments in the technical segment may be used for generating fast returns.

Some changes in selected stocks may be made in accordance with the market conditions. One point that needs to be kept in mind here is that 15% tax has to be paid on short term capital gains (where holding is less than a year) on every transaction.

Mutual Funds

A feel of investment in the stock market may be experienced straight away by investing in mutual funds. As per financial experts, diversification of portfolio is necessary when the investment corpus is quite large.

You should take into account the period involved when making an investment. You should hence make investments in suitable instruments depending on your expected requirements later. Suppose you have enough funds at the moment and you do not need the same for the next 5 to 10 years. In such a case, selecting equity-diversified schemes may be beneficial.

But if you expect fund requirement around two years after this investment, investing in debt oriented hybrid funds may be a better option. You may go for debt funds if you have less than a year before you may need money, as, along with the capital, guarantee of the security of return is also considered vital. One other way of investing is allocating 50% of investment fund to equity-diversified funds.

The rest of the amount may be invested in a planned way through systematic transfer plans (STP). If you plan 50% investment, you may gradually transfer amount to equity funds using STPs.

Any individual may choose STP option for a period of 6 months to 1 year for investment in 6 to 12 instalments. STP is more effective when the market is either at the top or there is a condition of uncertainly about the market moving up further.

Both Stocks and Mutual Funds

You should invest more in mutual funds compared to equities. As per experts, results may be better if you divide your investment amount of ₹5 lakh in the ratio of 2:3. Analysts suggest restricting the number of stocks for investment to 10. They together will be a crucial segment of your portfolio.

Those who have better risk taking capacity may put some money into mid cap stocks. However, this should be done only after detailed research, as normally small and mid cap stocks are associated with higher risks.

These stocks beat the Sensex and Nifty in a bull market but they also see deep declines during a slump. This happens because these are high beta stocks. For investing ₹3 lakh in mutual funds, experts suggest using some good equity-diversified fund.

Betting on equity-diversified funds may be quite beneficial as this is a safer investment as compared to stocks. This may be done through STP or by direct investment. While investing in mutual funds and stocks, it's very important to avoid investing more in the same sector or theme.

For instance, if you have invested in infrastructure fund and the things are not moving as expected, you may incur losses. Another point to be noted is that you should not get aggressive while investing and should also avoid mid cap stocks and funds, else the entire portfolio would become quite risky. If you have already invested in mid cap stocks, you should avoid investing in mid cap funds. Experts believe that while an aggressive approach may be adopted for investment in stocks, it would not be wrong to maintain a conservative stance on investment in mutual funds. A better way would be to use a systematic investment plan to invest regularly for a long period in a equity-diversified fund of a leading fund house. This would help you take benefit of market declines also. On an average, you would in the long run enjoy the benefit of compounding as well as that of market fluctuations.

❑❑

8

Safe Investment in Stocks is Possible

Safety with investment in stocks! This thought itself appears to be weird. Conventional wisdom says that investing in stocks is associated with maximum risk. How can somebody make such an investment safe? However, it is possible to minimise market risks related to investment in stocks. You may strengthen your investment process by adopting some simple techniques. Please keep in mind that the objective of investing in stocks is to earn money over a definite period of time and not to expect windfall profits overnight or within a week. Let's discuss some such techniques that may help us make our investments relatively safe.

Choose High Dividend Paying Stocks

Relatively high dividend paying stocks should be given preference. The dividend income is computed by dividing the stock price by the amount of dividend. For instance, Indian Overseas Bank paid a dividend of ₹4.50 per share for 2008-09 and its current price is ₹92. Thus, the dividend income is 5% approximately. Dividend is tax-free and hence this may be compared with the term deposits of banks. Sometimes, when you are not able to sell your stocks because of market conditions, you may possibly receive some payments towards final dividend or interim dividend. GNFC, Andhra Bank, Vijaya Bank, Castrol and Hindustan Unilever are some of the high dividend paying stocks. The point to be noted here is that the amount of dividend depends on financial performance and cash requirements of the company.

Stocks with Low PBV

Choose stocks that have relatively lower Price-to-Book Value (PBV). Book value per share is computed by dividing the total of capital, reserves and other amounts by the number of outstanding shares. PBV is then calculated by dividing the market price by book value. Generally, high growth companies have better PBVs. However, occasionally even some companies having good fundamentals are found to have lower PBVs. A lower PBV for a company may indicate its market cap to be lower than its net worth. This, in normal circumstances, indicates a higher intrinsic value of the share. Examples of companies with low PBVs currently include Federal Bank, Syndicate Bank, Karnataka Bank, GSFC, Gujarat Alkalies and Shipping Corporation etc. A high PBV indicates the company's net worth to be much lower than its market cap and hence investors should be generally wary of companies with higher PBVs.

Avoid Buying at Highs and Lows

Do not invest at 52-week highs or lows. High priced stocks may start falling after reaching the top. It's likely that the price of a stock after reaching the top goes up further only to a limited extent. Similarly, nobody knows how much further down a stock may go after it has reached its lowest level.

Buy Stocks of Well-managed Companies

Sometimes, investors, out of greed, put their money into companies that are not properly managed. But, the prudent advice is that you should choose stocks of only well-managed companies, even if they have lower return potential. This makes your investment a bit safer. Examples of well-managed companies include Reliance, HDFC, Infosys, Wipro, NTPC, Mahindra & Mahindra, State Bank of India and other public sector banks. After making investment, you should periodically review the same and take further steps based on their performance only.

Investors should watch out for sectors that may have

better demand in future. Based on the same, you should invest in the leading companies in those sectors. For instance, if you feel that the government is going to make a lot of investments in near future in infrastructure, power, energy and pharmaceuticals, you should keep a watch on the stocks of companies in those sectors.

❑❑

9

A Company's Report Card Reveals the Position of Its Share

Every game has some rules and some practices. If you have not learnt the art of following the basic principles, you would not be able to attain the desired dividend even if you follow the rules. Investors should go through the annual report of a company before choosing its share for investment. However, this is still not followed because of lack of clarity or people just turn a blind eye to the same.

We ignore the importance of this document and at the same time, we do not pay attention to the purpose for which the same has been created. The annual report is prepared to serve the information needs of shareholders, lenders, financial analysts, economists, customers, suppliers and promoters. Here are some useful steps that may help you safely walk through this haze and focus on the important points of the annual report. This annual report provides you the information beyond the report card on performance.

What to Read?

Considered as the primary document for investment, the annual report of a company outlines the management's perspective on future plans and its vision for the organisation. This not only provides information on company's operations but also indicates its financial health and broad strategies. Referred to as the investment thesis prepared based on the past performance of the management, this report contains the information that may not be obtained by normal deliberations on the company affairs. The report covers details about operational modalities of the company and hence, analysts suggest that you should study the same in detail to learn about the company's core capacity and to make a judgement whether it would be able to sustain itself in the current competitive environment.

This will help you make an inference easily whether the company would be able to raise capital for its expansion plans through adequate funding without selling its shares. However, the annual report should not be taken as the sole criterion for decision on investment. There are other sources also for information and they also should be paid attention to along with the annual report, while making an investment decision. There may be difference in managements' thoughts and ideas and the quality of disclosure for different companies. For this reason also, it's natural for the annual reports of different companies to be inconsistent.

Consolidated Value

Separate from the annual report, quarterly results do not contain balance sheet figures and cash flow statements. Also, it is optional to get the same reviewed by independent auditors. Hence, it becomes difficult to assess the strength of a company just by looking at its quarterly results. Compared to quarterly results, the annual report becomes special because of consolidated reporting. Companies have the option of not disclosing consolidated results in their initial three quarters. As such, they lack the impression of completeness.

Many a time, the performance of subsidiary units of a company may have a significant impact on its financial health. Quarterly results usually don't come under the purview of audit and hence you may not depend on these figures entirely. Analysts suggest that the annual report should be read along with quarterly results to have a more comprehensive picture of the company.

Quarterly reports provide you a way to analyse whether the management has fulfilled the promises made in its annual report. If they have failed in doing the same, you may exit from your holding of shares of this company without waiting for the annual report at the end of its business year.

Though all the sections of the annual report should be gone through thoroughly, most of the analysts opine that we should start with the section containing management thoughts and analysis so as to get an idea on the status of the enterprise, challenges and the promoters' perspective on its performance and strategy in the developing business environment. The financial statements should be deeply analysed next. Lastly, you should go through the balance sheet, profit and loss account and cash flow statement.

Value of Quarterly Results for Investors

A quarterly report of a company is the account of its performance during a specific quarter. Announcement of results is an obligation for the companies as per their agreement for listing with the stock exchanges. These reports are made public in the months of January, April, July and October.

The quarterly earnings report generally contains non-audited financial results, overview of operations and mention of future business prospects. Earnings report includes items such as net income, earnings per share, earnings from continuing operations and net sales. This may help you gauge the financial health of the company and its business environment.

Estimates for Upcoming Quarters

Some companies use these reports to also provide their estimates for future. This is called guidance. This is the management's estimate for the business operations for the next quarter and financial year. Guidance is important for the purpose of determining the financial expectations of the company. If a company's quarterly results match with its previous guidance, it reflects the proficiency of its management. If a company's estimates and its actual results have wide differences, it clearly indicates that you can't have much confidence in its management in future also. These are the inferences that short term investors many a time take into consideration for buying or selling shares of a company.

Marrow of Company's Performance

The quarterly results provide good indication of a company's performance. That is the reason that analysts and investors watch out for the same. Generally, analysts express their expectations based on estimates. The company's performance is evaluated taking all these estimates into account. The fact is that it's quite difficult to properly estimate its income. Thus, the projections made by brokerage houses for the company's income may be slightly more than the actuals. It's not easy for the companies themselves also to make accurate forecast for the same.

Investment Strategy for Results Season

Impact of the results of companies even on the price of their shares becomes visible with the release of their reports. If the result is above expectations, the price of the share goes up. If the same is closer to or lower than expectations, the price of the share may see a decline also. If the figures for a company are below expectations continuously for several quarters, it is possible that the company is facing some problems. Short term investors may formulate their investment strategy based on quarterly reports.

Long term investors may, by looking at these reports, get an idea about the operations of their companies. It is also necessary to go through the past performance of a company to evaluate its share. If the management has already declared the business plan of the company for the financial year, the quarterly reports may give the investor an idea of the quantum and speed of progress in its plan. Investors should also be careful to ensure that the company has not cooked up the figures. For instance, a company may try to inflate its profits for a quarter by adding up previous quarter profits and related expenses. Besides, it may even resort to selling its products on discount towards the end of the quarter just to meet the projections. In such a case, it becomes difficult to get the real picture of the company's performance.

Investors may get access to the quarterly reports through newspapers and business channels and on the website of the company.

❑❑

10

Groups of Stocks Listed on BSE

BSE has categorised its listed stocks in groups A, B, T, S, TS and Z. Besides this, some groups, including F and G, have been created for categorisation of securities.

Why are Stocks Categorised in Groups?

Generally, investors do not have complete information about every stock. In order to help them, exchanges categorise their listed stocks in grades based on their merits and deficiencies to enable investors to get some idea of their basic qualities while investing or trading in them.

How are the Stocks Categorised into Groups?

The stocks are categorised based on their market cap, trading volume, results, historical profits, dividends, shareholdings and some similar criteria. The stocks in the group 'A' are considered by the investors and the analysts to be the most reliable. The most important criterion for inclusion in this group is market capitalisation. Presently, a total of 216 stocks are included in this group. The stocks have to consistently maintain their strength to keep their position safe in a group, as many a time, stocks are shifted from one group to another. Some may get included in a group while some others may get removed. Stocks under BSE IndoNext Index have been included in the group 'S'. This index was created by the BSE on 7 January 2005. This S group includes stocks of some other groups also. Besides, companies having capital base between ₹3 crores and ₹30 crores and listed only on regional exchanges are also included in this group.

What Kinds of Stocks are Included in 'Z' Group?

BSE had created this group in the year 1999. The stocks of the companies that failed to comply with the exchange's listing requirement are included in this group. Also, the companies that are insensitive to their shareholders' concerns and the companies that have failed to make necessary arrangements for dematerialisation of their shares are included in this group. The stocks that do not find place in groups A, S or Z are included in group B. Before March 2008, the stocks in this group were segregated in groups B1 and B2; they have now been merged into a single group. T group contains stocks that can be bought and sold only on trade-to-trade basis. Stocks that belong to IndoNext index and are restricted to trade-to-trade segment are included in TS group. Fixed income securities are kept in group F and government securities come in group G.

❑❑

11

Rights Issue, Stock Split and Open Offer

Under rights issue, a company offers its existing shareholders new shares to raise capital. Usually, these shares are offered on discount (less that current market price). Existing shareholders may buy shares under rights issue in proportion to their existing holdings. For example, if a company announces 2:5 subscription rights issue, it means that the shareholder will have the right to buy 5 new shares for every 2 shares held. This will be applicable in the same proportion for larger numbers also. The shares released through rights issue can be traded after listing just like normal shares.

Stock Split

In this process, a single existing share is divided into

multiple shares thereby lowering the market price of a share proportionately. At the same time, the face value of the stock is also proportionately reduced. For instance, if a company announces to split its share having face value of ₹10 in the ration of 5:1 and the current market price of the same is ₹2000, the split would bring down its face value to ₹2 and its market price to around ₹400. Usually, companies resort to stock splits to increase trading in their stocks.

Stock Buybacks

Promoters generally use two methods to increase their stake in the company - slowly buy company stocks in the open market or provide the existing shareholders the option to sell their shares to the promoters at a specific price. The second process is called 'buyback'. In a buyback process, the promoter offers the shareholders to sell their shares by a specified date. While this increases the stake of the promoter in the company, the stake of the general public comes down. This puts a positive pressure on the price of the stock. Generally, buyback is considered to be favourable for the company as this indicates that promoters have full faith in their plans and the future of the company.

Open Offer

Just like rights issue, this is also a method adopted by the companies to raise capital. In an open offer, a company provides its existing shareholders the option to buy its shares at a price lower than the current market price. It's different from rights issue in the sense that shareholders are free to immediately sell the stocks received under rights issue whereas the stocks bought through open offer can't be sold immediately.

An open offer takes place if any of the promoters of a company wants to increase his stake or if non-promoters increase their stake in the company to 15% or the company is going to de-list from the stock exchange.

An open offer provides an exit route to existing shareholders. The company has to make a public announcement for open offer. When an acquiring company increases its stake in the other company to 5% or 10% or 14%, it needs to disclose its holdings at every stage to the target company and the stock exchange.

Once the total holding in the other company reaches 15%, the acquiring company has to announce an open offer. As per rules, the acquiring company is required to make an open offer for at least 20% additional shares. The price for the open offer should not be less than the average price of the share for the last 26 weeks.

What are the Requirements for Making an Open Offer?

The company making an open offer has to make a public announcement for the same. This announcement must include the offer price, number of shares to be acquired from the public, purpose of acquisition, identity of the acquiring company, future plans and time period for the open offer. The acquirer has to make payments for the shares acquired within 15 days from the date of closing the offer. For any delay, the acquirer is required to pay interest on the amount to the shareholders.

What is the Difference Between Open Offer and Rights Issue?

The purpose of both an open offer and a rights issue is the same - to collect funds. However, whereas the company or the promoter has to spend money in the case of an open offer, the process is quite simple for a rights issue. Often, the rights issue price is lower than the prevailing price of the share in the stock exchange. In the case of an open offer, the price is fixed based on the average price for the last six months. This offer price is usually higher than the prevailing market price. This higher price is a motivation for the current shareholders to sell their shares.

Open offer decreases the holding of general shareholders in the company while the rights issue increases their holdings on account of increase in the number of shares.

❑❑

12

Buyback's Funda

Buyback refers to the repurchase of shares by the company that issued them. By doing this, the company reduces the number of its shares in the market. Besides increasing the return per share, this move also enhances the returns on company's assets.

This also helps in improving the balance sheet. For an investor, the buyback means change in his holding in the company. Buyback is also sometimes referred to as shares repurchase and usually this indicates a jump in the price of shares.

How is Buyback Done?

A company may repurchase its shares through tender offer or in the open market. In the first case, the company issues a tender offer with details of the number of shares proposed to be bought and indicative price range. The investor interested in accepting the offer has to submit an application duly filled indicating the number of shares he is ready to tender and the expected price for the same. This form has to be submitted to the company. In majority of the cases, the price for the tender buyback offer is higher than the market price. As per SEBI regulations, if the company accepts your offer, it has to inform you within 15 days from the date of closure. The other route available to the company is to slowly buy its shares directly from the open market.

Where to Find out Details?

All the details related to buyback offers are available with the stock exchange, as companies are required to inform the exchange about all such proposals.

Why are Companies Going for Buybacks?

There may be many reasons for the same. Sometimes, companies engage in buybacks when they find the prices of their stocks crashing in the market. In other situations, this may be done to utilise surplus cash available with the companies. However, there is no example available where this has been resorted to for avoiding a takeover.

What is a Lot and what is a Margin Call?

In fact, unlike a cash market, stocks in a forward market can't be bought in arbitrary numbers. The exchange decides the minimum quantity for each stock to be bought. This very quantity or number is known as 'lot'. All the stocks are bought in lots only in the forward market. Though there is no set rule for the same, the price of a lot of stocks is usually around ₹2 lakhs.

What is Margin in a Forward Market?

Obviously, buying stocks in lots is a costly business. Hence, stockbrokers provide margin facility to their customers. Under this facility, an investor has to pay only a specific percentage of the total cost based on the standing of the stock and the broker pays the balance amount. Generally, the margin that the investor has to pay ranges between 20% and 30% for different stocks, the balance 70-80% provided by the broker as credit.

What do Long and Short Mean?

Being in a long position means buying stocks and going short means selling stocks even when you don't hold the same, by taking credit from your broker.

What is a Margin Call?

Suppose you take a long position for April for a lot at the rate of ₹5000. One lot of NIFTY has 50 units. That means, you need to pay ₹2,50,000 for the entire lot. Your broker asks you to deposit 30% as margin money. You accordingly deposit ₹50,000. The balance of ₹2,00,000 is provided by your broker as credit on your position. Let's assume the market starts falling after that and NIFTY reaches a level of ₹4000. That means your position is now valued at ₹2,00,000 only. If NIFTY goes down further even a little and you refuse to increase your margin money, your broker may incur loss even if the position is closed. Hence, in such a case, the moment NIFTY goes below 4100 level, your broker would ask you to deposit additional margin immediately. If you fail to deposit the amount before NIFTY reaches 4000, your broker would immediately close the position by selling the lot to ensure that he recovers the credit extended to you.

❑❑

13

Circuit & Value Averaging

Circuit is a mechanism to halt uncontrolled one-way trades in any index or stock in a particular trading session. For instance, if the circuit limit for a stock is 5% and it closed at ₹100 in the previous session, trades in that stock have to be restricted today within the range of ₹95 to ₹105 only.

How is the Circuit Decided?

The circuit levels for a stock are determined with the help of the historical data on fluctuations in its prices, average daily trades and fundamental strength of the stock. There are four levels of circuit - 2%, 5%, 10% and 20%. Different stocks are assigned different circuit levels based on their history.

How does Circuit Work?

There are two kinds of circuits - upper circuit and lower circuit. When a stock hits its upper circuit, there can be only buying and no selling in the stock. Similarly, when a stock hits its lower circuit, there will be only sellers and no buyers.

Are all Stocks Subject to Circuit?

Except the stocks involved in the forward market, circuits are applied to all other stocks to rein in their unanticipated rise or fall. The stocks traded in the forward market may undergo any levels of fluctuations on a single day. The trading does not stop for such stocks.

What is the Policy for Applying Circuit to Sensex and Nifty?

Both kinds of circuits are triggered for indexes in three stages - 10%, 15% and 20%. Once a circuit breaker is triggered for an index (Sensex or Nifty), trading in other indexes are automatically also halted. The circuit breaker when triggered brings about a coordinated trading halt in both spot and forward markets.

If the market falls by 10% before 1 PM, trading halts for one hour. If this fall takes place at or after 1 PM but before 2:30 PM, trading is stopped for half an hour. And if the market declines by 10% at or after 2:30 PM, there is no impact on trading activities i.e. it continues uninterrupted till 3:30 PM.

If the market falls by 15% before 1 PM, trading halts for two hours. If this fall takes place at or after 1 PM but before 2 PM, trading is stopped for one hour. And if the market declines by 15% at or after 2 PM, trading is closed for the remainder of the day.

When the market falls by 20%, trading is closed for the remaining day. In such a case, the Ministry of Finance often releases a statement and the government comes in action immediately.

What is Value Averaging?

Value averaging is an investment strategy that works like a rupee cost averaging in terms of steady monthly contributions. In value averaging, the investor sets a target growth rate or amount on his portfolio each month. Then, he adjusts the next month's contribution according to the relative gain or shortfall made on the original asset base. The main aim of value averaging is to acquire more shares when prices are falling and fewer shares when prices are rising. This is what happens in rupee cost averaging. In this process, you try to bring down the cost of acquiring stocks by buying further stocks later when the prices are at low levels. Over a long period running into many years, this value averaging helps in improving returns. Systematic Investment Plan (SIP) is the most significant instrument for the same. You may avail the benefit of value averaging for your monthly investment by investing in equity and mutual funds through SIP.

Assessment of Loss

The biggest potential risk with value averaging is that as an investor's asset base grows, the ability to fund shortfalls may become too difficult to deal with. One way around to this problem is to allocate a portion of assets in fixed income funds. Under this option, you may rotate money in and out of equity holdings as required to attain the targeted monthly return. This way, instead of allocating cash in the form of new funding, cash may be raised as part of fixed income and allocated in higher amounts to equity holdings as needed.

It's almost impossible to predict market tops and bottoms. However, investors may be benefitted by utilising different levels for their investments.

A majority of investors are aware of the concept of rupee cost averaging or systematic investment plan (SIP) of mutual funds. In this, you invest a definite amount at regular intervals. In the corridors of investment, value averaging is considered to be a more mature concept. Here, it is expected from the investor that he would keep adjusting his investment amount depending on the market trend (rise or fall) in order to reach the target value for the fund.

❑❑

14

How is Technical Analysis Performed?

We need to decipher the charts before we try to understand technical analysis. There are four kinds of charts - line charts, bar charts, candlestick charts and point and figure charts. Among them, bar charts are the most popular and most of the analysts use them.

How is Bar Chart Prepared?

A bar chart has a collection of vertical lines known as 'bars'. Every bar has one small horizontal line on each of its sides. Each bar depicts four values. The top of a bar indicates the highest price for the stock on a specific day while the lowest tip reflects the lowest price on the same day. The small horizontal line on the left of the bar indicates the opening price and that on the right side depicts the closing price for that day.

How is Bar Chart Prepared?

A bar is plotted for each day taking days on x-axis and price on y-axis and thus, a collection of such bars creates a chart. The bars for the days witnessing price drop (horizontal line on the left being higher than the line on the right) is coloured red or black and those for the days when price jumped (horizontal line on the left being lower than the line on the right) are coloured green or white.

What is the Importance of Volume in Technical Analysis?

Volume refers to the number of shares transacted. Technical analysis is actually a science to read the psychology of the entire market. Hence, it's natural that a proper inference of this psychology may be drawn only when more and more of people take part in the same. Prices for stocks having lower volumes are often controlled by just a few operators.

What is a Trend Line?

The straight lines drawn by connecting highs and lows for every day in the bar chart of a stock are called 'Trend lines'. Chartists draw the line through the highs to get the trend line for a falling stock whereas the trend line for a rising stock is drawn through the lows. In order to get more accurate results, the lines are drawn through dense areas of highs or lows for many days instead of using highs or lows for a single day.

Trend line is a trader's best friend. This has become a popular saying 'Trend is the best friend'. A trend breakout indicates that the direction of stock's movement is set to change. In other words, if a stock price is falling and suddenly the price crosses the line drawn through the highs and goes further down, it indicates the price will start trending higher. On the contrary, if the price of a stock or index crosses the trend line drawn through the lows and goes further up, it is time to exit high positions.

Meaning of Stop Loss in Charts

Stop loss is the price point of a stock or index at which the trade position is to be closed. Thus, in a chart of a stock with rising trend, the point at which the price crosses the trend line and moves down is the point of stop loss. Similarly, in the case of trades for a falling stock, the point where the price crosses the trend line to move up is the point of stop loss. When the stop loss is dynamically moved up and down based on the price, it is referred to as 'tracking stop loss'.

❑❑

15

What are the Basic Rules of Investing?

An individual investing in the stock market is the investor. Everybody should exercise prudence while making investment decisions. Here are 10 basic rules relating to investing:

1. Do not invest your entire savings in stocks only. For instance, if you have ₹1 lakh, you should invest only ₹25,000 in stocks. You should start with 25% only.

2. Instead of investing in the stock of a single company, put your money into stocks of different and well-reputed companies. For instance, you may select one stock in IT sector, second in banking, third in infrastructure and fourth in telecom or cement or steel etc. But all these stocks should be from well-reputed companies.

3. PAN (Permanent Account Number) and Demat account are essential for trading in stocks.

4. For trading in the stock market, choose a broker who has good reputation and quality services. He should have information on all the movements in the stock market. You should also ensure that the broker is duly registered.

5. Don't get misguided by tip culture. People may offer you advices to buy various new scripts of different kinds. Their prices may appear to be going up for a while but such investments without proper thought may result in disasters.

6. If your relative, friend or neighbour has made good money by selling some stock, please do not harbour any misconception that you also can make a fortune by buying and selling the same stock.

7. Never invest in a company just based on rumours in the stock market or news in media or hearsay. All the information about a company can be found on the website of the company. Take a decision only after making a proper research.

8. Investment is a long-term game. Day trading is just speculation that involves quick buying and selling within a single trading day. Hence, be conscious of the difference between investment and day trading. Day trading is quite risky. You may lose your entire savings in the same.

However, if you are able to master day trading, this may even become your full-time career.

9. Whenever you buy a stock, buy for a long-term investment. If its price is low today, it may even go up in future. Still, if you are getting a good profit on your holding in between, you should book the same. Sell your stock with at least 50% profit. If you have bought stocks of some not-so-reputed company, you should be ready even to bear loss.

10. The stock market is quite sensitive. It gets impacted by all kinds of incidents like changes in American economy, political events, inflation, earning results of companies, Asian markets, impact of industries etc. Hence, it keeps fluctuating constantly. You have to just keep yourself updated on the status of your stocks, not the index. If your stocks belong to good companies, they would go up again.

Success of an Investment Hidden in 7 Rules

You may be able to avoid failures and achieve success if you understand the fundamental realities of the stock market. Here are seven basic rules of investing.

- **First Rule:** When the market enters a bear phase and prices drop considerably, buyers lose enthusiasm and the investors in fact keep themselves away from the market in such a situation. However, the truth is that this is the opportune time when investors should enter the market and collect stocks slowly as and when they become available at attractive prices. Just think over, should you buy or sell when the index is at 21000? And, should you sell or buy when the index is somewhere between 8000 and 10000?

- **Second Rule:** Invest in a company, not in the stock market. The market chases away those who keep running after the price movements. On the other hand, those making their investments based on the performance and track record of companies do not get scared of the market movements. There are several factors that have impact on the stock market but there are very limited elements that may influence a company's performance. Hence, you should maintain your focus on the company, not the stock market. Your friends may keep watching the stock market movements while in reality, the stock market does provide good returns for good companies. A fresh example of the same is the case of Satyam that was marred by the famous scam and was later acquired by Tech Mahindra resulting in sharp rise in the price of its stocks.

- **Third Rule:** Decide whether you want to invest or speculate. Usually, people talk of investing in stocks and then start following the rates from the very next day after investing. Consequently, they are always worried after making an investment and later blame the market for their mental restlessness. The market is in any case going to remain volatile. That is its nature. How can it remain still with so many news and reports overwhelming it every morning? But you can surely be stable. Yes, for attaining success in the stock market, it is essential that you as an investor tread your path accepting both the truth and the reality.

- **Fourth Rule:** 'Profit is what you book'. In other words, profit or loss in books in the stock market may be a truth but not reality. The prices of your holdings may go up in a bull market and decline in a bear market, but this reflects your profit or loss in books only. Investors should fix a limit for their fulfilment with regard to return on stocks based on the returns normally available on traditional investments. This actually means that investors should book profits on their stocks at an appropriate time. Similarly, they should book loss also at appropriate time and at appropriate level. This decision has to be taken by the investors with prudence based on the circumstances. They should not wait for infinite gains and similarly they should not wait endlessly for the stocks to recover from their declines. Instead, they should accept the loss when situation does not improve and invest the remaining amount in some other stocks.

- **Fifth Rule:** 'Listen to everyone but do what you want'. In the stock market you always pay attention to what others say and what others do and you try to follow them. You would open the door to success in the stock market the day you stop blindly following others. Till the time you are part of the crowd, you would keep buying at the same time when others are buying and you would sell when others start selling their stocks. The key to success here is - 'buy when others are selling and sell when others are buying'.

- **Sixth Rule:** Don't get emotionally attached to any stock. One should feel contented with reasonable returns. Many a time, you feel satisfied with 8% to 10% of return on your fixed deposit with a bank or a company. While one particular stock may make your investment double within a month, the other may take 6 to 12 months for the same. But it's not necessary that this gets repeated every time. You should not let yourself get attached to any stock on permanent basis. Nevertheless, in some exceptional situations, good stocks may be left for your descendants as part of your testament.

- **Seventh Rule:** Equity stocks are the best investments in terms of returns. History has proven that out of various investment options of the world, investments in equity have always given the highest returns. Equity is also unique in the sense that it may even turn your investment into zero. This truth must to be accepted by the investor before putting his money into equity stocks. The other aspect of this truth is also that the investors who invested ₹10000 in the market for stocks like Wipro and held on to the same for 27 years have seen their investment growing to over ₹200 crores. That's why investment in equity is considered to be risky. The higher the risk, the greater the return!

❑❑

16

Beware of These Pitfalls While Investing

The recent global recession and the resultant mauling have taught the multinational companies and wealthy investors some invaluable lessons that they may utilise for protecting their investments when they encounter similar storm in the future. Here are the lessons:

Keep an Eye on Your Net Worth

It's essential to maintain a balance between income and loans. You may save your portfolio from heavy loss during market slumps if you exercise restraint over your spending and credits. An investor should have a clear idea of the difference between a good and a bad loan and should make a robust plan for repayments so as to avoid heavy interest expenses.

If an individual spends 30% of his take-home salary towards repayment of loans, he may soon get into trouble. You may keep home loan out of the purview of this list, as EMI payments would one day make you owner of that house. This is considered to be a good loan. However, the loans that you need to keep in control include car loan, personal loan, outstanding amount in credit card account etc.

The logic behind the same is that you spend 30 to 40 per cent of your salary towards your lifestyle and other household expenses and if you take out another 30% for repaying loans, it would become almost impossible to achieve your financial goals.

Don't you Dare Predict Market Movement!

Many investors try to gauge stock market movements. They believe that they will be able to enter the market at lower levels and exit the same at higher levels. But, we all know how many times this actually happens. In financial planners' opinion, it's not possible to predict in which direction the market may head the next moment. Many investors lose their money attempting to do the same.

There are many investors who enter the market during a bull phase and then, once they run out of capital, keep agonisingly looking for ways to exit from their investments. In fact, the right strategy would be just opposite of the same, as they put money into the market at high levels instead of low levels and hence, it takes a long time to recover the capital.

Diversification is the Right Strategy

Investors should keep in mind that their portfolio diversification may save them from unforeseen market slumps. The strategy of diversification should be adopted for investments in both mutual funds and stocks.

Secondly, you should set a sector-war limit for investment. Also, maintaining a proper balance is very necessary while investing in large cap and mid cap stocks. If a person is unable to keep a constant eye on stocks, he should go for a portfolio that includes only mutual funds; he may alternatively avail the services of portfolio management services. This would help the investor recover his capital and also earn faster returns.

Systematic Plan: A Long-Term Strategy

Experts advise that investors should certainly abstain from making the mistake of stopping their Systematic Investment Plans (SIPs) for investment when the index starts falling. During a market crash, you should try to fix the problem in your portfolio relating to the same being inclined more towards any specific stock or sector and you should continue your regular investments during the period. Investors following a method of diversified and systematic investment under a long-term strategy would be successful in reaping good returns without being affected by market downturns.

❑❑

17

Invest in Small Chunks to Create Large Portfolio

It Takes Drop by Drop to Fill a Jar

Investment in equity i.e. stocks is even today looked at with concern in our society. But, if you really want to create a large corpus, there is no better way than investing in the stock market. Even a small investment in equity made with care for a long period always grows to a large sum. People generally believe that a large capital is required for investment in stocks. But this is not entirely true. A large sum may be created by just investing a fixed amount regularly in the market for a definite period.

Capital Accumulation

It's not very difficult to accumulate a large sum by investing in the stock market in small chunks. Suppose you are earning ₹40000 per month and you can invest 10% of your total income for a period of 30 to 35 years. In such a case, a large sum would be available to you by the time you retire. If you are 25 years old and you plan to retire at the age of 60 and you have 3-4 dependents in your family and your total monthly expenses is around ₹25000 and you wish to accumulate a large capital through investments in equity, you would need to work on a perfect investment plan.

Create an Investment Plan

You propose to raise money for your retirement. As you are still young, you may invest in equity. Let's say you can spare ₹5000 per month for investing in diversified equity mutual fund and you may continue this investment till the age of your retirement. You may later make changes in the same but, for the time being, let's assume you will continue with the same mutual fund till retirement. Even though you are investing in equity, this investment has minimal risk, as you are investing for 35 years. In the stock market, it's the short-term investment that has the maximum risk. For a long period of 35 years, there is just no risk at all. You may achieve an extremely attractive return on this investment. If we just take the example of the Sensex, it has provided a return of almost 15 to 17 per cent per year over the last 30 years from 1979 to 2009. As such, if you are investing for long term, you may safely assume a minimum return of 15% per annum on the same. Let's come to the main point now. Investors may experience difficulty in sparing that much amount during initial years. Though their responsibilities keep on growing over time, their salaries also increase along with the growth in their career and they may not find it very difficult to spare 5000 rupees per month towards investment.

How Much the Investment would Grow?

You may invest ₹5000 every month. This means you are putting ₹60000 into equity stocks every year. As you are investing for 35 years, you would be actually investing a total amount of ₹21 lakhs over that period. Assuming an average return of 15% per annum, you may get an additional ₹3 lakhs. That makes the total to ₹24 lakhs. Now, if we calculate return on this total amount at the rate of 15% per annum, that also would come to around ₹24 lakhs. Let's assume you receive a total sum of ₹50 lakhs. This estimate has been arrived at based on simple interest only. People generally think from this angle only, but it does not happen like this. This is just a simple calculation without using the formula for annual compounding of interest, and this can be done by anybody.

Magic of Compound Interest

Interest is not computed like this. Your amount may

change to crores if we use compounding of interest. Your amount would in fact grow to ₹7.43 crores approximately when computed properly. You may be surprised to see that whopping figure. This is the magic of compound interest. You get interest on interest and that keeps growing. The amount of interest may appear to be small at the start, but the same keeps growing over time and for a long period like 35 years, that interest amount may look to be unbelievable. Would you believe that by investing just ₹5000 per month, you would get around ₹1 crore towards interest only after 35 years; this amount is more than four times your total basic investment. This is all the magic of compound interest. This is why the great scientist Albert Einstein had called compound interest the eighth wonder of the world.

Enjoy after 10 Years

It's ok if you don't want to bear the pain of investment for such a long period of 35 years. You just invest for 10 years and quit. The amount accumulated with an investment of ₹5000 per month for 10 years may turn into a large sum in the next 25 years on account of compound interest. You may get around ₹2.12 crores in this case; this is ₹5.88 crores less than the earlier amount. There is a way out. If you want to invest only for 10 years and still receive a sum of ₹7.43 crores after 35 years, you will have to increase your monthly investment. You will need to invest an additional amount of ₹1450 every month. That means, you invest ₹6,420 every month for 10 years and leave it to grow for the next 25 years. That would ultimately grow to a sum of ₹7.43 crores.

The More is the Burden you Endure Early the More the Comfort you Enjoy Later

You would have understood the point by now that the more discomfort you endure during initial years, the more benefit you reap later. A person is generally in a position to invest more during the beginning years of his career, as the responsibilities are less and he has only a few dependents then. If he goes on to face challenges and invests that extra ₹1420 every month for initial 10 years, he saves himself from the next 25 years of investment and still accumulates the same mount. If you feel that this opportunity for investment was available only 5 or 10 or 20 years back, you need not worry. The opportunity still exists.

❑❑

18

Mutual Fund: An Easy Option for Equity Investment

For the investors who do not have the time and interest to keep a constant watch on the movement of the market, it may be dangerous to invest directly in stocks. Equity portfolio requires regular monitoring otherwise you run the risk of missing the chance of exiting non-performing stocks and entering good stocks.

For such investors, it may prove to be a better strategy to invest in equity through mutual funds. In the case of a mutual fund, the onus of monitoring the stocks rests on the fund manager. However, choosing the right funds for his portfolio is still the problem of the investor only. Selection of right funds based on the risk capacity, investment period and return expected is quite important.

The nature of the market also influences the process of investing in mutual funds. Both the routes are available for investments in mutual funds - as a lump sum investment or through systematic investment plans.

Mutual Fund Portfolio

Equity diversified mutual fund is a good option for better returns. You may also choose funds where the portfolio is neither inclined more towards large caps nor focussed on a sector having good return but associated with wide price fluctuations. They should definitely put money into midcap and small cap funds. Nevertheless, the proportion of different funds in the portfolio depends on the risk-taking capacity of the investor.

You need to also keep in mind some other points like checking whether the fund specialises in growth or in value. It's good to learn about various cap funds in the market, as the same would help you to figure out which are the funds more suitable for your portfolio and your style of investment.

❑❑

19

Strategies to Minimise Risk in Mutual Funds

Investment in mutual funds is generally said to be a safe option for investment. This is because experts manage them quite professionally. But, does that mean that mutual funds are entirely free of risk? No, it's not like that. Come, let's understand various dangers and risks associated with them and be familiar with the strategies to minimise them.

Fund's Poor Performance

Usually, investors expect their chosen funds to move with the same speed, if not better, as that of the benchmark. However, in many of the cases, their funds lag behind the benchmark and their hopes get shattered. This happens because not all the funds succeed in beating the benchmark index. This is the reason that the possibility of a performance weaker that the index is more realistic.

Market Risks

Mutual fund investments are subject to market risks and there is no guarantee or assurance that the objective of the fund would be achieved. Instances of fall in prices of equity funds and bond funds in the short run or in the long run are also results of market risks only. The stock markets have cyclic movements. There are two kinds of spells. We may see fast movement in the market at some time while the very next moment we may see the market dropping. A great past performance of a mutual fund does not provide any guarantee that the same will perform well in future also and give expected returns to its investors.

Over Diversification

Over diversification occurs when two or more investments overlap each other. A well-diversified portfolio consists of asset classes that are not too deeply related to each other and hence they are considered to supplement each other. Spreading your circle of investments in different sectors will help you prevent any close link between two investments and will also lower the risk of price movements to a great extent. This is because not all the industries or sectors move in the same direction at the same time. Over diversification or widening your investment discriminately will not help you much. Instead, that may surely become a reason for loss.

Costs

Even if a fund fails to make profit, the investor is required to pay fees and other costs for the same. Mutual fund investors have to pay many types of charges that come together in a package. This fee is used by the fund house towards marketing, distribution, processing, asset management costs and other administrative expenses. Nevertheless, there is good news for investors from SEBI that has ruled that no costs will be levied on purchase of any kind of mutual fund.

Change in Investment Strategy

Portfolio investment managers have to make changes in their strategy depending on the time and circumstances. In such a case, the mutual fund diverts from its original objective and style of investment. This usually happens when the fund manager makes attempt to improve the fund's performance using different strategies. This ultimately results in misbalancing the risk and return for the fund.

Management Risk

When an investment manager is unable to handle his portfolio effectively, the fund fails to attain its objectives. Besides, any change in strategy by the fund manager may also alter the style of investment.

Industry Risk

The industry risk arises in the case of a group of stocks

belonging to the same industry or sector. Any change in the condition of that industry or sector may create problems in that case.

❑❑

20

Investment Avenues in Debt

Any reduction in interest rates makes borrowers happy. On the other hand, this results in loss to the investors who have put their money into debt market to avoid risks. A declining interest rate is not the only risk for debt investors. Though investments in debt instruments are considered to be safer compared to other investments, there are some risks associated with them also. Investors should pay attention to the factors like risk, return and liquidity while putting their money into debts. Following are the investment options in debt:

Non-convertible Debentures

A number of issues of non-convertible debentures (NCD) have come out in the market recently. They are offering good returns. However, they also come with more risks compared to other popular debt instruments. The reason is that large companies are successful in collecting funds from wholesale market at low rates but raising money from small investors is generally a costly option for them. Majority of the companies trying to raise funds from the market through NCDs are medium sized. Usually, the redemption period for a debenture is 5 to 10 years. The rate of interest on the same depends on the credit rating of the issuing company. The interest is generally paid at quarterly or half-yearly intervals and the same is taxable. As an investor, you should first of all check the rating of the NCD. This rating can be found in the NCD prospectus. AAA rating is the safest. Often, the basis of rating is also explained.

Company Deposit

The safety and return in this case also depend on its rating. Company deposits and banks' term deposits are quite similar. Fixed deposit schemes of three years of top rated companies are currently offering return rate of 10-11% against the interest rate of 8-9% currently available on bank deposits for the same period. Investors should be wary of the companies that do not have good track record in payment of dividends. Besides, even the companies that are in control of the first generation promoters have higher risk. As a matter of safety, NCD is considered to be a better option than company deposit. Also, company deposits are considered to be less secure compared to term deposits of banks. Deposit Insurance & Credit Guarantee Corporation (DICGC) insures term deposits up to ₹1 lakh in a bank. Companies like HDFC, LIC Housing Finance, HUDCO and ICICI Home Finance keep raising funds regularly through fixed deposit schemes.

Small Savings Schemes

These are government schemes and are considered to be the most secure compared to all other investment options. They come with tax benefits but lack liquidity. Public Provident Fund (PPF) is the most popular instrument among these small savings schemes. Interest is paid at the rate of 8% per annum and the interest is computed with annual compounding. The government may even alter this rate. A PPF investment has a lock-in period of 15 years. If you invest ₹10000 every year in this account, you will receive a sum of ₹2.93 lakh on maturity based on the current interest rate. The amount received on maturity of a PPF account is tax-free under Section 80-C of Income Tax Act.

National Savings Certificate (NSC) provides a tax-free return of 8%. Interest is computed with half-yearly compounding. If you invest ₹1000 in NSC, you will receive a sum of ₹1601 on maturity after 6 years. Investors may include both PPF and NSC in their portfolios. The rate of interest on PPF is revised periodically whereas the same on NSC remains constant for six years.

Both the options have the issue of lock-in periods. If your money gets locked for a long period, you may not be able to capitalise on the opportunities coming up in the market. You may miss investments in equity market providing opportunities of great returns.

Liquid Funds

As the name suggests, liquid funds are better in terms of liquidity compared to all other debt instruments. The lock-in periods in liquid or liquid plus funds are minimal. They provide returns between 6 and 7 per cent and they may be encashed within 24 hours. They have liquidity similar to that of savings accounts. The major difference between the two funds is that of Dividend Distribution Tax (DDT).

DDT (including surcharge) is charged at the rate of 27% on liquid funds whereas the same is just 15% on liquid plus funds. If somebody has a large sum to invest, liquid plus fund is a better option. There is however risk also associated with the same; if there is too much of uncertainty in the market, it may be possible that the investor does not get any return and even has to lose a part of his capital.

❑❑

21

FMP, Though Risky, Is A Profitable Investment

Asset management companies, every year, issue a series of Fixed Maturity Plans (FMP) in the last quarter of the financial year. These are fixed-term income schemes for definite periods and mature on specified dates. Their term may extend from 15 days to up to 2 years or even more.

FMPs generally invest in certificates of deposit (CD), corporate bonds and money market instruments. Thus, a 13-month FMP would invest in 13-month bonds. That's why there is no interest risk in the case of an FMP. This means that the value of your investment would not go down even if there is a bounce in interest rates on corporate bonds.

Safe, Though Risky

This should be clearly understood that FMP is different from fixed deposits (FD). FD is quite safe. However, if the bank goes bankrupt, your FD may be in danger. However, there is a very remote chance of a well-capitalised bank going bankrupt. In India, bankrupt banks are generally taken over by larger banks.

On the other hand, an FMP carries more of credit risk as its maturity payment depends on underlying investment instruments of the schemes. That's why it is necessary that the scheme is understood properly before making an investment. It should be ensured that corporate bands that are part of the scheme are having AAA or AA ratings.

As such, you should ignore FMPs that do not pay attention to quality of portfolio in a bid to keep the return high. After the market crash of 2008, the Securities & Exchange Board of India has instructed mutual funds not to declare returns on their investments and portfolio.

Now, even mutual fund companies are getting cautious about their portfolios and returns on bonds. A point worth noting is that none of the FMPs proved to be defaulter during the financial crisis. All of them paid interest as committed.

Tax Benefits

Earnings on FMPs during 2008 used to be around 10-11 per cent. This has come down to 7-7.5 per cent now. FMPs that invest only in bank CDs give an annual return of 6.8%.

When compared with FD, the most significant benefit that is found in FMP is its tax arbitrage where taxation is applied based on slabs. If you fall in the high tax slab, you would pay 30.9% tax on a bond that pays you only 8%.

This means that 8% return of a bond would be just 5.5% after tax. Though this return looks attractive, it may effectively mean loss of capital if you consider real return, inflation and rising prices. That's why, though you must invest in them, the maximum focus should be on real return or return after taxes and inflation.

Hence, you should choose the debt options that are either tax-free or tax efficient. If somebody in a high-tax bracket, preferential tax on FMPs makes its return 1.5 to 2 per cent better as compared to FDs. Being a mutual fund scheme, they provide you income in the form of dividends or capital gains.

It's so because the tax on dividends and capital gains is much lower than the same for high-income brackets. However, you need to even choose one of the options - growth or dividend. If you are investing in an FMP with a term less than 12 months, you may consider dividend option.

At the same time, capital gains under growth option are quite high for some terms and the same eliminates any tax arbitrage. If you are picking some scheme for a period more than 12 months, you should select growth option. Even under growth option, choosing indexation option is better from the point of view of savings.

❑❑

22

Mutual Fund Evaluation Criteria

Both investors and the fund managers keep a close watch on the performance of mutual funds. Investors wait for the reports and information for making investment decisions whereas the fund managers have their remuneration linked to the same. The return alone on a mutual fund does not reveal the entire story behind the same; however, it makes comparison among investment options more meaningful. Hence, selection of a benchmark assumes a lot of importance. Return on an investment and the risk related performance of the same are more important for investors. There are some investors who do not get bothered by lower returns provided the risk associated with their investments remains low.

There are two ways to evaluate the performance of a mutual fund.

Sharp Ratio

Sharp ratio is a way to measure the risk-adjusted performance of an investment. This helps to determine the excess return on the investment earned by the additional volatility of its risky assets. Suppose an investment X generates a return of 12% and another investment Y earns 10% return. Which of the two is a better performer? The return of 12% provided by X appears attractive at first glance, but you need to consider the benefits associated with the two investments. Suppose the investment in X is risky whereas Y earns risk-free returns. In such a case, Y would provide a better risk-adjusted return. The return generated by X is not in proportion to the risk associated with the same.

Sharp ratio is arrived at by subtracting return earned on risk-free assets from the return on mutual fund or portfolio and then subtracting the same from standard deviation of the scheme. The return on the mutual fund scheme less the return on its risk-free assets reveals the excess return generated by the scheme in comparison to the risk-free asset.

This excess return is divided by the standard deviation of the asset to determine the sharp ratio or the additional return on account of the extra volatility associated with the same. The standard deviation measures a stock's volatility. The more the return on the stock deviates from its average return, the more will be its volatility. Assets having higher sharp ratio provide better returns in the ratio of the associated risk.

M Square

Is your investment rewarding you enough for the risk you are taking? Plunging in the stock market without paying attention to the risk-adjusted performance of mutual funds is considered to be imprudence. Modigliani or M-squared return is a hypothetical return that an investor would have earned in a timeframe had the fund's risk been adjusted to match that of a benchmark. This measures the return on the fund that the investor would have earned had he borne the same risk that the market index had. However, the results may be misleading when a mutual fund has altered the strategy on its investment style. Besides, a cloud of doubt is always there over whether the returns on the fund would be sustainable in future. Sharp ratio and Modigliani computation provide valuable inputs to investors. However, do not base your decision on the fund's performance alone.

23

How To Pick The Best Mutual Fund

Choosing the best mutual fund schemes for investment is an important step. It's not only important but special also. Picking mutual funds makes sense only when you have set major long-term financial goals. If you are investing for a short period like if you are investing in a liquid fund, it does not make difference which of the liquid funds you are choosing. There is not much of difference in performance of two different liquid funds. Pick the liquid fund that has larger asset under management (AMU) and that provides redemption facilities through phone or Internet.

Set Your Goals

The most significant initial step for investment is to define your goal for the same. It's entirely pointless to choose a good fund without that. You should understand the reasons for your investment like - how much time you may give to your investment and under what circumstances, you may alter your investment options. If you are clear about your goals, you would be able to choose right options for your investments. That only would also decide the amount to be invested in equity funds.

Homework is Necessary

Do some homework before making investments. Buy good large cap diversified funds. Do not buy opportunity funds, international funds and country funds as primary funds of your portfolio. All the funds in India are now free of entry loads. It means that you don't have to pay any fee for buying them. This is good as your entire money gets invested.

Keep Close Watch on Asset Management Fee

Once a fund gets a good start, it should attract investors in large numbers. And as its portfolio grows, its asset management fees should come down. Look for the better managed funds whose fees are lower than 1.9% per annum. There are many such funds in the market.

Portfolio Turnover Ratio is Important

Special attention should also be paid to Portfolio Turnover Ratio. Increase in this ratio indicates increase in total costs for the fund. The cost that is not visible to the investors is the brokerage paid by the fund scheme. This depends on the portfolio turnover and hence, the costs for the funds having lower turnover are low.

Special Role of AMC Team

The team of an asset management company also plays an important role. As an investor, you should look for an experienced team that has managers who have already gone through some business cycles. The managers who have not gone through market downturns may be unforesightful but those who have experienced extended market slumps may even be highly pessimistic. Hence, you should look for a team that has a mixture of both.

True to its Name

A fund should be really true to its name or objective. If a fund is said to be a large cap fund, it should not invest in mid-caps and small caps only because large caps are not in favour currently. It's your decision to invest in large cap fund and your fund manager must honour this truth.

Harmony of Thoughts

Some fund houses are quiet and restrained compared to others. It's you who has to decide whether the ideology of a particular AMC matches with yours. For instance, Templeton proclaims that Franklin India Blue Chip is a growth oriented large cap fund whereas Templeton India

Growth Fund is a value-oriented fund. It's up to you to find out whose ideology suits you.

Who is Managing the Fund?

Managing a fund is both an art and a science. The fund manager of any scheme definitely leaves his mark on the fund. However, some fund houses are capable of creating teams and system to handle a situation arising from a fund manager quitting his job. This system provides comfort to your mind.

Choosing a Better Index Fund

Avoiding well-managed index funds under the purview of long-term investments is difficult. Presently, all the fund houses claim that their schemes are performing better than index; you should however beware of such calculations. These fund houses do not include charges while projecting their performances. Hence, if you compute with costs included, you will find that many of the schemes are actually faring worse than the index. In such a case, if you are not looking for extra excitement, pick an index fund that comes with charges not exceeding 1% per annum.

❑❑

24

Why Are Mutual Funds Safe?

Investors are usually quite concerned about the future of companies, especially when they come in the spotlight or some news concerning them gets published. It's often heard that many fund companies are running in loss. Some of them are discussed about their being too small in size and their inability to run for long. Some other companies are in the news for their merger with other companies. Recently, Goldman Sachs, a very reputed American investment bank, went bankrupt. The same thing happened with Shinsei Mutual Fund. Shinsei Bank of Japan also had a large holding in the same. It's imperative for you to keep your reaction to such news under control else you may hurt yourself badly.

Volatility is Inevitable

Based on the assessment of the above companies, it may be said that some upheavals in mutual fund business will definitely be there. Coming days may see some volatility in fund business because of removal of entry load for mutual fund transactions and resentment of regulatory authorities over insurance business being carried out in the guise of ULIP. But, should regulators be really worried about the same? Majority of the analysts believe that these are common news doing the rounds in the industry. Investors should ignore them and focus on long term investments, as the market regulator SEBI will not allow any fund that has been launched with the objective of swindling investors' money, to stay in the market.

Investment in India Safe

A quick look at the history of Indian mutual fund industry makes it clear that this apprehension is baseless. There is nothing new in business upheavals in the fund management industry. During the last 20 years when the mutual fund industry came into existence and grew to a level we see today, many of the promoters of such companies felt that some changes in their plans for the industry were necessary. Nevertheless, the investors had to bear loss on account of the same. Mutual fund industry in the country has seen some 56 companies in its history. However, at least 19 companies out of them could not sustain themselves for long. This means that at least one third of the asset management companies either closed down their business or managed to somehow exit from this business.

Long History of Acquisitions

In fact, AMCs that are functional and have investors possess enough value to be able to acquire another company altogether or acquire entire business or only fund business of another company. Despite this, there are many companies in the market that have gone through multiple acquisitions.

Regulators are Quite Effective

One reason for low level of apprehensions in the minds of investors in Indian mutual fund industry is that the mutual fund regulator is working very effectively. Investors' funds are held entirely separate from the operations of asset management companies. Till date, only two instances have come to light where investors had to face problems. One of them was the bankruptcy of CRB Mutual Fund during 1997. Promoters were running CRB fraudulently and even the regulators at that time were not so effective as they were expected to be. The other case relates to erstwhile Unit Trust of India. But this was a unique incident. The investors though don't need to have any kind of worries in the current regime because of the level of mutual fund business today and existence of a powerful regulator.

❑❑

25

Mutual Fund: Precautions

If you are not conversant with the ups and downs of the stock market, mutual fund is a better option for you. Thousands of mutual fund schemes are currently available in the market. Investors are confused where to invest their money. In the situation, picking the right scheme is necessary to keep your money safe and also to get a good return.

Which Fund should I Pick?

- These days, there are plenty of websites that provide information on funds. Do a proper research using those websites before making an investment.
- Look into the track record of a fund before putting your money into the same. Pick a fund that has a long and superior track record.
- Trust the fund house that is known for its process of

investment. Many people invest in funds just by looking at star fund managers. It's better to avoid that.

- For a long-term investment, it's better to stick to a scheme that is interested in diversified investment.
- The market has a straightforward funda - return always comes with risk. As such, if you make a long-term investment using the systematic route, this risk gets reduced.
- For a better return, one should strive to create a mutual fund portfolio with a balance among large caps, mid-caps and small caps.

Safe Return, without Risk

Those who do not want to invest directly in stocks and are also not happy with the low return on bank deposits should head to debt funds. This is considered to be a safe investment for long term. Those who wish to invest for short term have the option of liquid funds. These funds provide a return better than savings accounts. People investing in debt funds may buy government securities or corporate bonds through banks or bond houses.

Systematic Investment Plan (SIP)

For making money in mutual funds, it's necessary to invest, even if it is a small amount, for long term through systematic investment Plan (SIP). Making small investments every month on a fixed date would help you accumulate a good sum. Suppose you propose to invest ₹4000 every month. You may invest the same in four parts on four different dates. Fund houses provide multiple dates option for the same. While investors have to wait for the market to come down to invest in stocks, investment in mutual funds may be started any time using SIP. The net asset value of the fund increases as the market goes up. You hence get lesser number of units against your investment at that time. This way, your average return is maintained. Investments made through SIP are considered to be safe and rewarding when the market is going through wide ups and downs. You may this way achieve great returns by investing in good equity funds using SIP route. You may start your SIP even for ₹100 only. Now, the government has even banned the entry load.

Tax Relief

Investment in an equity linked savings scheme of a mutual fund not only provides the benefit of tax relief of ₹1 lakh under Section 80C of Income Tax Act but also better returns. The dividend and returns under this scheme are tax-free. This scheme is known as Equity Linked Savings Scheme. However, there are talks of this ELSS getting removed from the list of 80C when the new DTC comes in force in 2012.

ABCD of Mutual Funds

Kinds of Funds

- **Open Ended Fund:** There is no fixed term for schemes

coming under this category. The scheme provides the facility for the people to invest in the same any time.

- **Close Ended Fund:** Its term is fixed. This term is mentioned in the initial offer document of the fund. Nevertheless, the fund house may, with the consent of investors, alter the term based on rules. These funds are available with a lock-in-period of three years. Investors may still exit the fund by paying exit load.
- **Equity Fund:** Equity fund provides the best return in a bull market. If you are planning a long-term investment, equity funds are preferable.
- **Income Fund:** Contrary to equity funds, this involves lower risk. Here, the rate of return is quite low as compared to the same for equity funds.
- **Balanced Fund:** Diversification is taken care of in its investment. Hence, market risk gets reduced for this fund.
- **Money Market Fund:** This fund invests mostly in those fixed income instruments that mature in less than a year. This a better option for investing for short term.
- **Debt Fund:** This investment does not provide higher returns but keeps money safe. Debt funds earn well during the periods of interest rate upheavals.

26

Funds that Drew Attention of Investors

i. ETF Fund

Don't restrict yourself to stocks only when investing in the stock market. There are other products having returns similar to or better than that on stocks available with other names or in other forms in the stock market. However, investors do not pay proper attention to them because of their ignorance. The awareness about these products has now started to improve. The investment product in the name of ETF (Exchange Traded Fund) has many special features. This is traded on BSE and NSE on regular basis. Let's have a look at some such products.

These products are meant for long term planning. Not only that, they are unique in the sense that they provide high liquidity. Some of these products have surnames attached to them like BeES i.e. Benchmark Exchange Traded Scheme. Benchmark Asset Management Company, the first company to moot the idea of ETF, has started ETF in three assets viz. equity, index and gold. Besides being the frontrunner in this field, this company also has maximum share in the market. Other companies that have launched ETFs later include Reliance, UTI, Kotak Mahindra, ICICI, SBI and Quantum. These ETFs are available in Bank Index, PSU Index, Gold etc. in addition to NIFTY and Sensex.

❖ **NIFTY BeES:** When somebody invests in multiple stocks, the risk of volatility in income gets eliminated. But it's also a point as to how many stocks at all can be acquired with the investment of limited capital. But, NIFTY BeES is an ETF that invests in 50 scripts comprising the benchmark index NIFTY of the National Stock Exchange. Consequently, even the smallest of investors in NIFTY BeES effectively makes investment in all those 50 scripts. And hence, his risk gets distributed among 50 different stocks.

NIFTY BeES is also listed in the stock market just like other stocks and trades can be carried out in the same every day like normal stocks. Its price is quoted on unit basis. If NIFTY is at 5000, one unit of NIFTY BeES is priced at ₹500 (i.e. one tenth of NIFTY). If you hold 2-3 NIFTY stocks, it's possible that their prices go up while

NIFTY goes down. But NIFTY goes up only in the long run and hence, this product is turning out to be the best option for long term investors. Similarly, SENSEX may also be bought for long term investment. This is traded on BSE in the name of SPIcE; it's an ICICI product. Compared to your futures trades in NIFTY index, your trades in ETF (NIFTY BeES) of NIFTY would be cheaper and even less risky. You may even trade for a single unit. You also don't need to arrange margin for buying NIFTY BeES. The other product of Benchmark is 'Gold BeES'.

- **Gold BeES:** Firstly, the nature and propensity of gold are mostly opposite to those of equity. This makes gold a great instrument for hedging against equity. However, buying or selling gold in the form of ETF instead of physical form is a better means for dealing in gold for investment purpose. In our country, gold comes in handy to meet unforeseen financial urgencies. Gold is also required at many auspicious occasions in the family. You may accumulate Gold ETF buying one unit at a time and then convert the same into physical form when required. Not only that, the prices of physical gold and Gold BeES are almost same. You may even meet your needs of physical gold with money received from sale of paper gold. Gold BeES has many special features. It does not suffer attrition like physical gold and it also does not have the risk of theft. This gold is held electronically in Demat account like stocks. Costs involved in its trading is also comparatively less. Gold BeES is also quoted in units and its one unit is equivalent to 1 gm of gold. Physical gold attracts wealth tax whereas paper gold is free from that tax. Not only that, there is no security transaction tax also on the same.

- **Liquid BeES:** This product is also traded in the stock market. Liquid BeES is special in the sense that it is considered equivalent to cash, as it is accepted as margin money. If you trade in stocks, you may ask your broker to hold your funds meant for stock trading in Liquid BeES so that you keep getting return on the same. Dividend on Liquid BeES is paid on daily basis. Suppose you have sold some stocks of ABC Company and the amount has been deposited into your account with the broker. Till the time you need this amount for buying other stocks, you may invest the same in Liquid BeES and whenever you need, you may pay for fresh stocks by withdrawing Liquid BeES units and selling the same. This helps you get return on your idle funds in the form of investment in Liquid BeES. It's just true to its name. The NAV of Liquid BeES remains around ₹1000. The dividend paid on the same gets reinvested, thus making it grow. Most of the depository participants do not levy any fee on this. Its transactions do not attract STT also. It may be traded even for a single unit. There is no entry load and exit load for Liquid BeES.

Products of Benchmark Asset Management include Junior NIFTY and Bank BeES also. These products being in the form of ETF have the potential of minimum risk and maximum return in the long run.

ii. Gilt Fund

Gilt funds are the funds that invest in government securities. These securities are guaranteed by the government against any default. However, their rates also keep going up and down. This investment gets safely repaid on maturity; the return may be variable and hence the risk involved is minimal, if not zero.

Investments in gilt funds do not sink and ₹1 lakh invested in the same does not turn to ₹12000 and you get good returns also. During 2008, when investments in equity had turned negative, gilt funds had earned 7% to 24% within a year. Not only that, returns of 6% to 14% were achieved by them within 3 to 6 months only. Investments in these products are considered to be quite good for short terms. As the period of investment goes up, the return starts going down whereas in the case of an investment in stocks, the rate of return rises with time and the shorter the period the more is the risk.

Today, safety of investment is vital. Whenever you find threats on your investment, be it in equity or any other product, gilt fund comes in handy as a good investment option. However, you should remember that even in the case of a gilt fund investment, if you take your money out midway, it is possible that you incur loss on account of low NAV of the fund.

For whom is Gilt Fund Safe?

This fund is quite safe as it invests in government securities. Gilt fund is considered to be equivalent to bank deposits. Investments in gilt funds proved to be the best during 2008. When the entire world was facing liquidity problems and financial crisis, investments in these funds provided great relief to the investors.

It's good for the investors to keep a specific portion of their capital in gilt fund schemes as a separate asset class; this specifically applies to senior citizens, ex-servicemen and those people who do not want to take risk. At least gilt funds would provide returns better that the same you get when you park your funds in savings accounts.

iii. Shariah Index

Shariah index is an index based on the companies in which investments can be made in accordance with Islamic laws. Most of the Shariah indexes created till now are based on existing or underlying index. The companies included in such indexes are screened by a board that is well versed with the principles of the Quran.

How are the Companies Screened?

Every company is screened at two fronts - first based on the sector that the company operates in and then based on some of its operating ratios. For instance, all companies in a particular index whose business activities are connected to pork, alcohol, gambling, finance, tobacco, pornography, gold-silver and cash are excluded from the Shariah index.

Besides above, companies linked to advertising and media (excluding newspapers and a few other cases which are analysed on an individual basis) sectors are also left out of this index. Additionally, the amount of debt, cash and the revenue accrued from activities that are non-compliant to the principles of the 'Quran' are also taken into consideration.

For instance, a company having the ratio of debt to the market value of equity lower than 33% is considered to be compliant to the principles of the Quran. Similarly, if the revenues that come from non-permissible activities are less than 5% of total revenues, the company may be included in the Shariah Index. It's possible to increase the number of companies included in a Shariah index.

What are the Reasons for Creation of Shariah Indices?

In an essay on Islamic finance, Martin L Ross says Islamic law lays emphasis on the need to avoid usury and risk. Islamic law does not consider money as an asset and hence does not favour the practice of making money from money. This means that lending money on interest has been considered to be against the Islamic principles. Even sale of products whose existence is not certain is treated as a wrong practice. Typical examples of the same may be insurance products which somebody buys based on a future eventuality.

Is there any Shariah Index in India?

While Indian companies have been included in Shariah indices in the past, the first two Shariah indices based on the Indian stock markets were launched by Standard and Poor's in February 2008. They are known as S&P CNX 500 Shariah and S&P NIFTY Shariah. They have been created after screening the companies constituting the S&P CNX 500 and the S&P NIFTY.

iv. Gold Fund of Funds

The consecution of launch of new products in the world of mutual funds is now gaining speed. Asset management companies are presenting new kinds of fund schemes on regular basis.

Investors should ensure, based on their specific needs, that they make the best use of these new schemes. Recently, offer documents have been filed by fund houses for launch of a new scheme Gold Fund of Funds (FoF). We are going to explain here how investors may review these schemes to reap desirable benefits from them.

What is Gold FoF?

The Gold Fund of Funds is slightly different from regular mutual fund schemes. The fund of these funds is not directly invested in stocks, debt instruments and gold. Their portfolios consist of the funds that have such kinds of instruments.

The Gold FoF also has to invest in funds that invest in gold. This provides you an investment option in gold different from the common investment products.

Conventional Investment Options

As of now, Gold Exchange Traded Fund (ETF) is the only option for those wishing to invest in gold. The option of fund of funds is currently available only for debt instruments and equities. Gold Fund of Funds (FoF) will be a new kind of asset that will include other funds also. It's necessary to be aware of some points before making an investment in the Gold FoF. First, you already have the option of ETF to capitalise on the fluctuations in the price of gold. In such a case, what's the point in investing in new Gold FoF that also has similar features? The offer documents for Gold FoF that have been filed with the market regulator make it clear that these funds are going to make minimal investments in debt and money market instruments. That means that they will have slightly better returns compared to ETFs, though this can't be guaranteed. Overall, the return would depend to a great extent on the expertise of the fund manager. Another point that has to be kept in mind while investing in FoF is that the extra expenses incurred for this scheme should be commensurate with the investment. If that is not so, ETF would be a better option for investment.

Where will They Invest?

Till now, four fund houses have filed offer documents for Gold FoF and if, as per their proposal, funds investing in the stocks of companies engaged in mining of gold are also included in the portfolio in addition to gold ETF, it may be considered to be a great gold portfolio. This would not only help in capitalising on fluctuations in the price of gold but also make a positive impact on the return of the fund on account of the earnings and performance of those mining companies.

At the same time, this also needs to be considered whether the company launching Gold FoF is going to invest in its own ETF or is also exploring the options outside its funds family. Right now, the offer documents do indicate that fund houses are looking at both the options in this regard. Many asset management companies have proposed investment in ETFs within their fund families while many others are desirous of investing in external ETFs.

What should an Investor Do?

At the moment, many investors are making use of Gold

ETFs for investment in gold. As such, till the time a new fund scheme is available and its operational procedures for investment are well defined, people should continue with their investments in Gold ETFs. New Gold FoF should not form more than 10-15% of your portfolio. It's expected that these funds would be kept in the category of debt-oriented funds. In such a case, Dividend Distribution Tax (DDT) would have to be paid. Though the investors would receive tax-free dividends, they would have to bear indirect tax in the form of DDT. The tax liability on capital gains would depend on the period of investment in such funds. The income from investments for periods less than a year would be treated as short term capital gains and the same would be taxed as per normal income.

Capital gains arising over a period more than a year would be treated as long term capital gains and the same would be taxed at the rate of 20% with indexation and 10% without indexation.

v. Debt Mutual Fund

End of a financial year is generally the time when investors review their portfolio. Some people may feel this to be tiresome as only a few days are left for meeting the investment requirements. Some other people may use this opportunity to secure additional earnings. This may be a better opportunity, especially for investors in debt mutual funds, for availing great benefits.

Indexation Benefits

The profit earned by selling a mutual fund investment at a price higher than its cost is known as capital gain. The earning from an investment in a fund for a period less than 12 months is called short term capital gain while the same from an investment for a period over 12 months is categorised as long-term capital gain.

Taxes are applied at different rates for the above two gains and extra benefit is available for long term capital gains. This extra benefit is available in the form of indexation where the cost of investment is adjusted in proportion to the inflation for the period of investment. Indexation is arrived at on the basis of Cost Inflation Index notified by the tax department every year.

Double Benefit

The financial year end is the time for the investors to avail the opportunity of double benefit by using indexation. Double indexation benefit is available to the investments that do not require lock-in for two years; however, this must be for a period exceeding one year.

For instance, if a mutual fund is purchased during financial year 2008-09 and sold in April 2010, 2010-11 is assumed to be the sale year. Though this investment is held for a period slightly over a year, indexation benefit may be availed for the same for two years, thereby reducing the tax liability. Suppose a person invests ₹50000 in a debt fund at the rate of ₹10 per unit during March 2008 and is allotted 5000 units of the fund. In April 2009 (i.e. after 13 months), he sells his units @ ₹11.80 per unit. He thus receives a return of 18% on his investment. As the period of investment is more than 12 months, it will attract long term capital gains tax. The taxable amount has to be computed accordingly. In this case, the cost of investment has to be increased on account of indexation. The Cost Inflation Index was 551 for the year 2007-08. The year of sale was 2009-10 and the index for the same was 632. Thus, the cost of investment is computed to be ₹57,350 for taxation. As the amount received on sale was ₹59000, the long-term capital gains tax will be applied on an amount of ₹1,650 only.

Tax has to be paid at the rate of 20% on this amount. Thus, despite a good earning, tax on the same is saved because of indexation benefit. The entire amount becomes tax-free after double indexation.

❑❑

27

Shariah Funds

Shariah refers to the Islamic canonical law based on the teachings of the Quran and incorporates a clear framework for Muslims in reference to their financial and commercial activities.

While on one side, Shariah law pays attention to business and investments, on the other side, Shariah investment rules prohibit alcoholic beverages, gambling, pornography, abortion, human cloning, defence, conventional banks or insurance companies and most of the forms of entertainment. Industries connected to pork also have no place in this system. Benchmark Mutual Fund had launched Shariah BeES in the form of an ETF in March 2008. This is a passively managed fund that invests in securities which are constituents of S&P CNX NIFTY Shariah Index in the same proportion as in the index. For any investor who is ready for a low-risk investment, this passively managed fund is a good option; this may replicate the market and provide a return quite consistent with the same on securities representing the S&P CNX NIFTY Shariah Index. At the same time, Taurus Ethical is an actively managed diversified equity fund that entered the market in Match 2009. Equities in companies following the principles of Shariah are selected out of the list of S&P CNX 500 Shariah Index constituents. As both the funds are equity-based schemes, long term capital gains from them are tax-free while short term capital gains attract tax @16.99%. Neither of the funds comes under tax saving schemes. In order to avail the tax benefits under Section 80C of Income Tax Act, you would have to invest in equity linked savings schemes (ELSS).

> My mother is a senior citizen. She wants to invest around ₹1 lakh in a monthly income plan. She may take reasonable risk to enhance her income but incurring any loss of capital would be difficult. In the light of above, please suggest some schemes. A return target of 12% pa is desirable.

Monthly income plans come under debt funds category. Investments in these funds do have risks involved. The objective of an MIP is to provide monthly income by investing 80% of funds in debt instruments; however, the return is neither fixed nor ensured. Your mother is a senior citizen and her primary aim is safety of her capital. In such a case, you advise her to invest in Senior Citizen Savings Scheme instead of MIP. This would provide her a return of 9% p.a for a fixed period of 5 years; the return is computed on quarterly basis.

Please explain the process of investing in mutual funds through SIP. I want to make monthly investment of ₹10000 for around 5 years.

SIP permits an investor to systematically invest a fixed sum on regular basis. This provides the benefit of cost averaging. That means that when you buy mutual fund units on a regular basis over a long period, you automatically buy more number of units when the prices are low and less number of units when prices are high. This results in lowering of average unit cost and hence reduction in the risk of anomaly in your investment. Besides minimising the impact of uncertainties related to the stock market, this investment for 5 years in equities would be able to provide a good return. You may choose 2-3 funds like HDFC Top 200, DSPBR Equity and Magnum Contra.

I want to enter the stock market but I have to invest for a long term. I hence want to get an idea of capital gains tax. Kindly let me have some details.

A long-term capital gain is the gain stemming from the sale of stocks that have been owned for longer than 12 months. This is tax-free. On the other hand, gains from sale of investments owned for less than a year are called short term capital gains and tax @15% is applied on the same.

This rate is not advantageous for investors. Hence, investors should try to ensure that capital gains are converted to long terms to avoid tax. Investors have to trade in NSE and BSE for this. If an investor wants to avail this benefit on sale of stocks, he must trade through these two stock exchanges only. Another important condition is that the stocks, irrespective of the place where they have been bought, must be sold through these two stock exchanges only to avail the benefit of above rates.

Please guide me for investment in stocks. I want to invest in the stock market.

Regarding the stock market, it's common perception among people that only those people succeed there who are able to keep a constant eye on the market or who have expertise in the same or else it may be a losing proposition to stay long in the market. Stock brokers, financial advisers, stock analysts of brokerage companies and even so-called expert anchors on TV channels would advise you that long term investment in the stock market would not be advantageous. They would very much advise you to keep churning your portfolio of stocks and actively keep making purchases in the stock market to reap desirable benefits. They all are the people who want you to keep a constant eye on the scroll (moving band at the bottom of TV screen) on your TV screen. Also, be watchful of the ups and downs in the stock market even if they involve a few points only. They believe that time is the most effective weapon to make money in the market. Hence, it's important to focus on the appropriate moment. Here, it may be easy to understand what after all is the reason for their hurry. They want to keep you inadvertent with regard to long term investment; but this may prove to be a big mistake for you.

The best way to invest in the stock market is to buy stocks of the companies who are demonstrating balanced performance theoretically and are having constant growth in business. At the same time, invest for long term instead of buying for short term. Just make sure that those companies have transparent management and they have friendly attitude towards their shareholders. Warren Buffet is the most prominent example of the people making money this way. At the moment, he is the biggest investor in the world. He never attempted an aggressive approach to investing and always considered long term investment to be preferable. Currently, his wealth is estimated to be over US $ 150 billion. He had started investing with a very small amount and gradually accumulated this huge capital over a period of 52 years. An investor always puts his money into a company considering its performance and does not indulge in rapid buying and selling.

I want to invest a lump sum and expect a return better than that provided by a debt fund. I am ready to take moderate risk, with a maximum loss of 10% of capital. Can Monthly Income Schemes (MIP-Growth option) fulfil my goals? If not, please suggest other options.

MIPs invest around 10% of their portfolio in equities. This investment in equities helps them to perform better compared to pure debt funds during bull phases of the market.

In view of your desire to attain higher returns as compared to debt funds and your readiness to take some risk, you may consider investing in MIPs. However, do not invest your entire sum in one go; instead, invest the same in a systematic way.

Besides that, you may also bet on Arbitrage funds, as they provide returns similar to debt funds but are more tax efficient than MIPs and debt funds.

I am working for a private company and want to buy a house for myself. I want to invest in mutual funds to be able to buy a house costing around ₹20 lakhs. I am looking for a good return, may be around 12%, to enable me to book a house in six months. I have around ₹4 lakhs for investment. Where should I invest for 6 months?

Mutual fund investments are not meant for short term. For

a period of just 6 months, you should keep the fund in bank term deposits. Contrary to mutual funds, bank deposits ensure safety of your capital and also provide you a fixed return. In short, do not take any risk of losing capital or incurring loss.

❑❑

28

Important Share Market Terminology

1. What is Book Value?

The book value of a company or an item is the amount that would be received on its sale in the open market at a specific time. Roughly, this may be arrived at by subtracting depreciation from the cost of acquiring. For instance, suppose you buy a car for ₹5 lakhs and 15% depreciation is applied on the same every year, its book value after one year would be ₹4.25 lakhs. In Britain, book value itself is considered to be the net asset value for a company; this is arrived at by subtracting the values of patent and goodwill from total assets.

What is Book Value of Equity Per Share?

The minimum value of a company's equity is referred to as the book value of equity per share. In other words, the value arrived at by adding the price of common shares of the company and cash reserves and subtracting the amounts spent towards dividends and share buyback from the same is what is known as BVPS. BVPS does provide an estimate of the current value of a share but it does not indicate its future prospects. Hence, it's not right to make an accurate evaluation of a share on the basis of BVPS.

What is PBV?

Comparison of the market price of a share against its book value provides an indication how costly or cheap the share is against its real value. PBV ratio is used for that purpose. On the lines of Price to Earnings Ratio (PE), PBV i.e. Price to Book Value Ratio provides an idea at what multiple of its real value is the share trading in the market.

What is Return on Assets?

Return on Assets (ROA) is an indicator of how much profit a company is making on its invested capital. This in a way reflects the efficiency of the company's management. Return on assets to a large extent depends on the sector in which the company is operating. Hence, it's difficult to get a clear picture of the company until its Return on Assets is compared against the same for another company in the same sector.

A higher ROA indicates that the company is capable of making better profits on low investment.

2. Share Arbitrage

Arbitrage is the practice of taking advantage of the difference in the price of a financial product between two markets. The person or institution taking advantage of arbitrage i.e. the arbitrager buys a product in a market at a lower price and immediately sells the same at higher price in the other market. Suppose an arbitrager buys 100 shares of a company in the spot market at the rate of ₹10 per share and sells the same in forward market at the rate of ₹10.10 per share. Assuming there is no cost involved in the above trades, the arbitrager earns a profit of ₹10 in the process.

What are its Basic Conditions?

Arbitrage is not possible when the law of one price for every product is in existence. It means that arbitrage opportunity arises only when there is a difference in price. For arbitrage, it's necessary for the product to have different prices at some point of time. Arbitragers sometimes use different products with identical cash flows. Using this strategy, they take advantage of the difference in prices of the financial product between spot and forward markets. For this, the spot price of the product should not be more than the forward price plus its cost of carry.

How Many Types of Arbitrage are There?

There are many types of arbitrage like Merger arbitrage, Convertible Bond arbitrage and Reverse arbitrage. Merger arbitrage involves entering into deals at higher price for the stocks of the company being acquired and at lower price for the stocks of acquiring company. In this strategy, the arbitrager plays with the difference in price i.e. the spread between the market price of the stocks of the company being acquired and the offer price of the stocks of the acquiring company. Usually, the forward price of a financial product is more than its spot price. However, occasionally forward price goes below the spot price and arbitragers get an opportunity to make money. They sell the product in spot market and buy the same in forward market. This is called 'Reverse Arbitrage'.

What are the Risks Involved in Arbitrage?

Generally, arbitrage involves fairly low risks, though some events may enhance the risk of loss. For example, let's assume an arbitrager takes a position in merger arbitrage but the acquisition does not take place. The arbitrager may incur heavy loss in such a situation. Arbitrage involves buying stocks in one exchange at lower price and selling the same in another exchange at higher price. However, the difference in the prices of stocks is maintained for a long time. The risk of loss arises if an investor is unable to execute both purchase and sale transactions at the same time.

What is the Current Situation?

In recent times, investors are taking more interest in the financial products that involve relatively lower risk arising from the conditions of too much of uncertainties in the economy and the stock market. For sometime, even arbitrage funds are receiving fairly good investments and they are also performing well.

3. Broker as Player

In the stock market, intermediaries and institutional brokers are known as 'Players'. Brokers, dealers, banks, merchant bankers, mutual funds etc. are all covered in the category of players.

- **Open Order:** If an investor places an order with his broker but the same remains to be executed and has still not been cancelled, the order is called Open Order.

- **Open Bidding:** If an auction permits anybody to bid for the same, it is called Open Bidding.

- **Open Ended Mutual Fund:** Any investor may invest anytime in this kind of a fund. The NAV (market price) of the mutual fund is regularly published in newspapers and there is no fixed maturity period for the fund.

- **At the Opening Order:** If an investor directs his broker to enter into a deal right at the opening of the market, it is called 'At the Opening Order'.

- **Overnight Loan:** A loan extended by a bank only for a night is known as 'Overnight Loan'. This loan is repaid to the bank next morning.

- **Gun Jumping:** When buying or selling of stocks of a company occurs based on information that has not yet been disclosed to the public, it is referred to as 'Gun Jumping'.

- **Hot Money:** The capital that is often quickly moved from one country to another country for investment is called 'Hot Money'. The sole purpose of this kind of investment is to profit from the differences in interest rates and exchange rates between such countries.

- **Hot Issue:** If a public issue is in heavy demand among investors and the same is being heavily traded at premium in unauthorised market, it is referred to as 'Hot Issue'.

- **Buy and Hold Strategy:** If an investor buys stocks and holds the same for long term to earn long term capital gains, it is referred to as 'Buy and Hold Strategy'.

4. What is Price Earnings Ratio?

This is in fact the most elementary criterion for determining the valuation for any share. In other words, it may be understood in a way that this ratio indicates how many times of the annual earning of a share an investor is ready to pay for that share. To be straight, PE of a share is actually the number of years in which the value of the share would become double of its present cost. Suppose a share at any point of time is priced at ₹100 and its earning per share is ₹5. That means its PE ratio would be 20. It indicates that, if the conditions remain the same, the value of this share of ₹100 would become double in 20 years. That means the PE ratio of that share is 20 at that point of time.

What is the Relevance of PE in Valuation of a Company?

PE only indicates how bullish or positive the market is on the share. No inference may be made on the basis of one PE alone. For arriving at a conclusion, this must be compared against some other PE ratios. Firstly, historical PEs of the same company for the last 5-7 years; secondly, PE ratios of companies operating in the same sector and thirdly, PE ratio of benchmark index like the Sensex. Two inferences may be made if the PE for a company is quite high - first, company's stock price is too high relative to its true value and hence, it's overvalued; second, the market knows that the growth rate of the company is going to be very high in coming days and hence, people are bidding for the stock even at high prices.

What are Trailing PE and Forward PE?

Trailing PE is the ratio of the stock price and its earnings for the last 12 months. Similarly, Forward PE is determined based on the projected earnings for the next 12 months.

How to use PE to Determine Real Value of a Stock?

Often, conditions are not always the same for a company. A company's earnings may go up or down every year. Besides this, any fresh issue of stocks through FPO would increase the total number of its stocks. All these have impact on its earnings per share. If a company has been historically maintaining a PE of 30 for the last 5 years and suddenly, the PE falls to 20 because of market slump, the stock can be considered as cheap. However, if the company involved is Infosys and there is an atmosphere of confusion about its earnings because of probable slump in the United States, you may not call a PE of 20 to be cheap at first sight.

5. Dividend: Right Pocket's Money in Left Pocket

In our environment, free items receive a lot of attention. The moment something is made available for free, people become too thirsty to get the same. Something similar happens in the case of mutual fund schemes. Companies mislead people with regard to dividends and investors are not able to realise that.

What Companies Do?

Dividends appear to be attractive to investors. Investors feel that they would make good money with the help of dividends. People believe that when Infosys pays dividend, the company effectively takes money out of its pocket to fill their pockets, thus itself getting poorer to make them rich. But, is that what really happens? Perhaps not. The companies in these funds do not do anything except transferring money from your right pocket to your left pocket. In reality, neither these companies become poorer by paying dividends nor you become rich by receiving dividends. This is actually your own money that comes back to you. In other words, the value of your investment goes down to the extent of dividend received by you.

Mutual Funds: Beware of Misconceptions

There was a time when we had only Unit-64 scheme of UTI as an avenue for mutual fund investment. It was in 1987 when for the first time, a non-UTI fund came in the market in the form of SBI Mutual Fund of the State Bank of India. Private sector entered this field for the first time in 1993. At present, the size of mutual fund sector is around ₹4,85,000 crores. Even after that, mutual fund still remains a misunderstood investment option. Investors usually have erroneous conceptions. In fact, when companies go on launching funds one after the other, they themselves create such misconceptions. Distributors are only interested in selling the funds. In the entire process, excessive advertisements and attractive commission to distributors create an environment where investors are unable to pay attention to the real scope of returns. They get entangled in dividend etc.

Maintain Single Folio Number for All Transactions

In our environment, there is a convention to maintain many kinds of numbers. Bank account number, password, PAN, tax deduction number, collection account number, customer identification number and mutual fund folio number are all separate. Though there is some operational compulsion for the same, there is one number that you should not change. That is mutual fund folio number. You may get into trouble if you change folio number. Hence, please do not change your folio number, especially when you are investing in different schemes of the same fund house. In fact, single folio number should be maintained for all transactions in mutual funds.

AMC Allots the Number

Investors are allotted folio numbers by asset management companies. This number is unique for every fund house. You receive this number from the fund house when you make your first investment in one of its mutual funds. This is different for every mutual fund. You can't have a single number for all fund houses. However, you may use a number allotted by a fund house for any other investment with the same fund house. The benefit of this system is that you wouldn't have to face any difficulty in recollecting the folio number every time you make an investment with that fund house.

Why are Multiple Numbers Maintained?

People rarely use their existing numbers while making fresh investments, even when they have already been allotted folio numbers. What actually should happen is that you use your existing folio number only when you make a fresh investment with a fund house where you have already invested earlier. You should fill that number carefully in the mutual fund application form. This would save you from maintaining multiple numbers. You wouldn't have to keep a note of all those lengthy numbers of your accounts. Keeping a single folio number also helps in carrying out transactions in future. Another benefit is that the same number may also be used for buying any additional fund in a specific scheme. This becomes even more important for the sale of funds etc. This number may be quite helpful when you submit two separate applications for selling a fund.

6. Some Common Words in Market

- **Exchange Value of Money:** When the value of the prevailing currency of a country is fixed against a foreign currency to enable exchange of currencies, that value is called the 'exchange value of currency'. This value depends on the internal purchasing power of the currencies of the two countries.

- **Money Inflation:** Inflation is the condition in which the intrinsic value of a currency declines and prices of goods go up. That means, there is increase in supply and availability of money and credit. This is also referred to as money expansion.

- **Money Devaluation:** This is done by a government. This process only brings down the external value of the currency. When the exchange rate of the currency of a country is lowered in respect of foreign currencies, the process is referred to as 'devaluation of money'.

- **Creeping Inflation:** This is the soft form of inflation. When the level of prices in an economy rises at a very slow pace, it is referred to as 'Creeping Inflation'. Economists keep the annual increase of 1% to 3% in this category. This condition saves the economy from inertia.

- **Record Date:** For announcing bonus shares, rights shares or dividends, companies declare a cut-off date when their registers would close. Only the holders of securities as recorded in the register of a company as on its declared cut-off date are treated as real holders. This date is referred to as 'Record Date'.

- **Refund Order:** If share allotment is not processed for an application for shares, the company has to refund the entire amount along with the application. The document that the company sends for refund is called 'Refund

Order'. The refund order is in the form of a cheque, a demand draft or a banker's cheque and the same may be usually encashed at par value at the local branch of the issuing bank.

- **Dividend:** Dividend refers to that part of a company's profits that is distributed among its shareholders. This may be either tax-free or taxable. This is earning for shareholders.
- **Dividend Rate:** The amount of dividend paid on one share of a company, when expressed along with the record price of the share is referred to as Dividend Rate. This is usually expressed as a percentage.
- **Dividend Securities:** The securities on which investors receive dividends as return are called 'Dividend Securities'; examples are parity stocks, preference shares.
- **Zero Rated Debenture:** No interest is directly paid on this category of debentures or bonds. Instead, they are sold on discounted price when issued and are redeemed at full price on maturity. The discount in the price of the bond/debenture at the time of issue is treated as the interest on the same.

7. Funda of Primary and Secondary Market

We often come across the terms like primary and secondary markets when we enter into trades in stocks. Let's learn about primary and secondary markets.

When a company, in order to meet its requirements, issues new shares or debentures directly to investors for raising capital, it is said that the company is raising funds from the primary market or that the shares are being sold in the primary market. When a company issues new shares or debentures through Initial Public Offer (IPO) in the market, it is said that capital is being raised from the primary market.

A company may raise capital by issuing fresh shares in the primary market even after IPO. Once an IPO or public issue of a company is executed, the company gets listed in the stock exchange and its shares are then traded through the stock exchange.

While in the primary market, companies sell their shares and investors buy them without the involvement of the stock exchange, in the secondary market, institutional and retail investors trade shares of companies among themselves. That means trading in shares in the secondary market is carried out through the stock exchange whereas the companies sell their shares directly to the investors in the primary market.

8. What is Breakout?

When the price of a share breaks the Trend Line upside or downside, it is referred to as breakout. It is called positive breakout when trend line is broken on the upside and negative breakout when the trend line is broken on the down side.

Breakouts are often used for closing long positions or to

create short positions. For instance, if a trader has entered into a long position in Reliance and a negative breakout is encountered in the same at any specific price, it indicates that the trader should exit his long position and enter into a short position. On the contrary, if the trader is already holding a short position, he should cover his position and enter into a long position the moment a positive breakout is encountered.

How to Identify a False Breakout?

Many a time, a stock returns below the trend line after going through a positive breakout. Similarly, negative breakouts are also many times proven to be false. Such breakouts are called 'false breakouts'.

To protect himself from a false breakout, a trader should follow the strategy of setting up the breakout level as stop loss the moment he enters into a trade based on a breakout. As such, it's necessary to pay attention to volume to identify a false breakout. In a genuine breakout, the volume of the share is usually quite high compared to its average volume. Breakouts not associated with volume are mostly false.

What is Triangle Formation?

When the price of a stock continuously makes lower tops and higher bottoms, its trend line takes the form of a triangle. In such a situation, the possibility of a breakout exists on both upper and lower sides. However, in any case, such a breakout on any side is usually strong. But, for such a breakout to be genuine, it is necessary that the same occurs within the two-third part by length of the triangle. If it occurs somewhere inside the last one-third, it is not considered to be a genuine breakout.

9. What is Bonus Issue?

When companies accumulate large cash reserves, they issue bonus shares. By doing this, a company makes additional payments to its shareholders as dividends. In other words, a major portion of the cash reserves of the company gets transferred from the books of the company to the personal accounts of the promoters, as they are usually the biggest shareholders of the company.

Why do Companies Make Bonus Issue?

When shareholders are issued shares free of cost in proportion to their existing share holdings, it is referred to as 'Bonus Issue'. For instance, if a company issues 2:5 bonus shares, it means that you would receive 2 free shares for every 5 shares held by you.

How does it Make Difference?

In a way, nothing! It's common belief that bonus is very advantageous for the shareholders. However, price-wise it does not make any appreciable difference. Suppose you have 100 shares and the company has announced issue of 1:1 bonus shares. Your holding thus goes up to 200 shares.

Similarly, if the company had 1 crore shares in the market earlier, this number goes up to 2 crores now. But, the market cap of the company can't go up in the same proportion.

Hence, ex-bonus i.e. once the bonus shares enter the market, the share price in principle goes down by half. It's a different matter that practically, the price does not drop exactly by half but comes to a level near that. No convincing or basic reason may be attributed to the same. First, investors get an impression that the company issuing bonus shares is quite strong in respect of its cash reserves and second, the amount to be received as dividend doubles. They have a role in increasing the demand of company shares.

At the same time, the drop in the price of company's shares after a bonus issue in the same proportion results in increase in their daily trades.

What is the Impact on the Face Calue of the Share?

The face value remains the same after a bonus issue. In fact, the main difference between a stock split and a bonus issue is that while bonus issue results in price drop but no change in face value, stock split brings down the face value in the same proportion.

10. What is QIP?

Under QIP (Qualified Institutional Placement), a listed company issues equity shares, fully or partly convertible debentures or any securities other than warrants. They may be converted to shares later. However, QIP is meant only for Qualified Institutional Buyers (QIB).

QIP is a means to provide shares to some specific people or groups of people. However, this is different from the process of issuing preferential shares. QIP is simpler as compared to other methods for issuing shares. This does not involve much of formalities. SEBI has to be informed before making this issue.

Why was this Started?

QIP system was put forward by the market regulator SEBI in the year 2006. Before this, listed Indian companies were too dependent on foreign capital. In fact, Indian companies were facing a lot of problems in raising capital from the domestic market. They depended on Foreign Currency Convertible Bonds (FCCB) and Global Depository Receipts (GDR) for raising funds. SEBI introduced QIP to minimise or in fact eliminate that dependence.

What are the Rules Related to QIP?

A company has to meet certain criteria to be eligible for using QIP. Firstly, the company has to be listed. Secondly, the shares of the company must be held by common investors. Its quantity is fixed in the agreement executed at the time of listing. In addition to that, the company, while bringing out QIP, has to issue at least 10% of the securities to mutual fund schemes. If the issue size is up to ₹250 crores, there must be at least 2 buyers. If the issue size is more than ₹250 crores, there must be at least 5 buyers. No one buyer can buy more than 50% of the value of the issue. Also, issue can't be allotted to any QIB that is linked to any of the promoters of the company.

Why was QIP in the News Recently?

Real estate company Unitech had issued QIP. Unitech was in need of funds. The company raised ₹1,620 crores through QIP. The share of promoters in the company came down to 51%.

11. What is Dual Listing?

Dual listing is the process where a company gets itself listed in stock exchanges of different countries. When two companies located in two different countries enter into a business agreement, their stocks get listed in both the countries through dual listing. The main point here is that the stocks of both the companies can be traded in the stock exchanges of the two countries. In other words, if a condition of dual listing were included in the agreement to be executed between Bharti Airtel and MTN, stocks of Bharti would be available for trade in Johannesburg Stock Exchange whereas stocks of MTN would be available in a domestic stock exchange.

How Many Companies have Dual Listing Currently?

There are many complexities in dual listing and hence this is not so popular. However, there are many examples of dual listing. Stocks of Royal Dutch Shell are traded in the stock markets of England and the Netherlands. Stocks of BHP Billiton are available for trade in Australia and England. Similarly, stocks of Rio Tinto group are traded in the markets of both Australia and England. Stocks of Unilever are traded in the markets of England and the Netherlands.

Is Dual Listing allowed in India?

At present, dual listing is not permitted in India. This requires substantial changes in the company law of the country. Besides, rupee will have to be made fully convertible. Under dual listing of a company, an investor may buy its stocks in one country and sell the same in another country. This requires Rupee to be fully convertible. Foreign Exchange Management Act (FEMA) will also need some amendments. Besides that, stocks being traded in foreign currencies can't be traded in domestic markets without the permission of Reserve Bank of India.

12. Foreign Institutional Investor (FII)

Foreign Institutional Investors (FII) and fund houses make significant impact on the trend of stock markets. When FIIs start selling, the index comes down and their investments result in good upturn in the market. The stock market regulator SEBI makes available on daily basis the details of investments by FIIs in equity and debt markets. Market players use this information to gauge the trend of investment by the FIIs. The impact of FIIs on equity market is so powerful that domestic buyers and fund houses are unable to stand up to the forceful moves of the FIIs.

In view of the significant role of FIIs in the movement of index, investors also should keep a watch on their investments in the domestic market.

Who are the FIIs?

They are the financial institutions or companies that invest in financial markets of different countries other than that where these organisations are based. The trend of investments by the FIIs is unpredictable and that's why, this investment is referred to as 'hot money' in the market.

Buying by FIIs

What happens when investments by FIIs increase in domestic markets? We may expect a rise in the real effective exchange rate (REER) in such a case. This rate is used to determine the value of currency of a country in terms of currencies of other countries. Even the impacts of inflation are adjusted in this. In simple words, increase in FIIs investments results in upward trend in the market. Especially, the stocks where FIIs have invested get jumps. Besides, increase in investments by FIIs also makes Rupee strong. This also has impact on domestic exports as these products become costlier in foreign markets. Rise in investments in domestic markets also results in better liquidity, thus raising the possibility of inflation. Economic stability may get impacted by these related activities.

Sell-off by FIIs

When they are in need or when the conditions are not conducive, FIIs suddenly start selling their holdings. This was observed during the market slump. When FIIs had made heavy sell-off and domestic markets were licking the dust, even small investors had to endure heavy loss and their equity portfolio had come down to just half in value. In view of the increasing impact of investments and sell-offs by FIIs, investors should also keep a watch on the their movements and global affairs. This would help them in taking investment decisions.

13. Fear Index?

Volatility Index is also known as Fear Index. Novice investors should be aware that this index reflects the volatility of the market. This indicates to what extent that specific index is going to record ups and downs during the next 30 days. For instance, if VIX for National Stock Exchange is currently at the level of 40, it indicates that the equity market may go through ups and downs to the extent of 40% during next one month.

In a stable market, VIX is usually below 10. A high VIX level indicates that the investors have got struck with fear. You may use this fantastic tool as the first indication of an impending bull phase in the market. If volatility goes below 20, you may consider your investment reasonably safe.

❑❑